MARGUERITE BOURGEOYS

The author wishes to thank the following persons who helped in the preparation of the manuscript and the illustrations: Danielle Dubois, Cécile Duplain, Stéphanie Manseau, Eileen McGurk, Joyce Roberts, Nathalie Simard and Monique Tremblay.

Front cover illustration: Charles Vinh, *Montreal's first school opened by Marguerite Bourgeoys in 1658,* 2008 (photo: Normand Rajotte)
Back cover illustration: Miraculous statuette of Virgin and Child (photo: Normand Rajotte)

All photos of which the credits are not identified belong to the collection and archives of the Marguerite Bourgeoys Museum.

Saint Marguerite Bourgeoys did not write an autobiography. She did, however, leave behind certain writings. Among them are reminiscences, letters and instructions to the sisters of the community she founded. These fragments have been collected and translated into English in *The Writings of Marguerite Bourgeoys* published in Montreal by the Congrégation de Notre-Dame in 1976. Many of the section headings and all the quotations attributed to Marguerite Bourgeoys come from that source.

Bibliothèque et Archives nationales du Québec and Library and Archives Canada cataloguing in publication
Simpson, Patricia
Marguerite Bourgeoys: Brave Beginnings
ISBN 978-1-897092-03-3
1. Bourgeoys, Marguerite, Saint, 1620-1700.   2. Canada - History -To 1763 (New France).
3. Nuns - Québec (Province) - Biography.   I. Title.
BX4700.B76S543 2009   282.092   C2009-941578-x

Legal Deposit: 3rd trimester 2009
Bibliothèque et Archives nationales du Québec
© Éditions Fides, 2009

Éditions Fides acknowledges the financial support of the Government of Canada through the Book Publishing Industry Development Program (BPIDP) for their publishing activities. Éditions Fides also wishes to thank the Canadian Council for the Arts and the Société de développement des entreprises culturelles du Québec (SODEC). Éditions Fides is funded by the Government of Quebec tax program for publishing, a program managed by SODEC.

PRINTED IN CANADA IN JULY 2009

Patricia Simpson

MARGUERITE BOURGEOYS

BRAVE BEGINNINGS

FIDES

Detail of a freestyle image inspired by an 1852 portrait of Marguerite Bourgeoys attributed to Antoine Plamondon.

"In 1640 I gave myself to God"

"Can we not take our birth from that time when God inspires us to give ourselves to Him knowingly and of our own free will?" Marguerite Bourgeoys asked. It is not surprising, then, that when she took up her pen to record her memoirs or to write all that she left of an autobiography, she always began at the same point: the moment at which she was radically transformed by what she called a "touch" of grace. There are several accounts of that event in Marguerite's surviving writings, all set down in the final decade of her long and adventurous life in response to situations of the time. They are not simply descriptions of a historical event; they are the introduction to what she saw as the action of God in that life. Across more than fifty years, her memory of the moment that transformed her life remained vivid — so vivid that she must often have revisited it in prayer. In her most complete account she wrote:

In on Rosary Sunday, I went to the procession at the Dominican Church where there was so great a number of people that the cloister was not large enough. So we crossed the street and passed in front of the portal of Notre Dame where there was a statue in stone above the door. And glancing up to look at it, I found it very beautiful. At the same time, I found myself so moved and changed that I no longer recognized myself. When I returned home, this was apparent to everyone.

This description deals with a very precise moment in Marguerite's past that was, in her view, directed toward the future. It points forward to the path she would take away from the cloister, following what she believed to be the example of Mary, Christ's mother and first disciple. At the same time, it also contains elements that suggest something about the deep and strong roots from which Marguerite's life and work would grow.

A land of poets and merchants

In the course of her life, long even by 21st-century standards, Marguerite Bourgeoys journeyed far in space, to the America that was still very much a New World in her time and to the very frontiers of that New World. Her journeys of the spirit were just as far reaching, from the cloister that had once beckoned her to a form of religious life lived in the midst of the ordinary struggling people of her day, rather than among the high and mighty. She was at the forefront of efforts to educate the poor and, especially, to educate girls and women. But her own roots lay deep in the rich past of the city and region in which she was born, Troyes, the ancient capital of Champagne in France.

Troyes can trace its beginnings back to Roman times and owes its name to the Celtic tribe the Romans conquered and Christianized. Because of its position on the great trade routes linking Europe and Asia, Troyes, in the Middle Ages, was an important commercial centre whose economy was enriched by the large trade fairs that, for a time each year, made it a truly cosmopolitan city. But it was also a city with a rich cultural life, in part as a consequence of the prosperity these fairs provided. Troyes gave to the world a system of weights, but it was also the home of one of the greatest writers of medieval romance and of one of the greatest of Jewish scholars, both of whom are known by their connection with the city, Chrétien de Troyes and Rachi de Troyes.

Marguerite grew up in a city of beautiful churches: her parish church of Saint-Jean-au-Marché, Saint-Madeleine with its exquisite carved screen, Saint-Rémi where her parents had been married, Saint-Urbain founded by the pope from

Troyes, Saint-Nizier with its roof of glazed tile, the Cathedral of Saint-Pierre et Saint-Paul. The architecture, sculpture and stained glass that inspired her and supported her prayer in these churches can still be seen today. Champagne was also a region where, at least since the Middle Ages, women had played a prominent role, among the greatest of them the abbesses of the great Benedictine monastery of Notre-Dame-aux-Nonnains over whose portal Marguerite looked at the statue that so inspired her.

"There is great hope for a child"

Marguerite was the seventh of the thirteen children born to Abraham Bourgeoys and his wife Guillemette Garnier. She was preceded in the family by two brothers and three sisters and by another child who died in infancy. No bells would have rung out for her baptism in her parish church of Saint-Jean-au-Marché on April 17, 1620, for it was Good Friday that year. In an age when a quarter of all babies died before the age of one year, baptism took place as soon as possible after the birth of the child.

Marguerite's father was a master candle maker. His shop, selling candles and various by-products of candle making, occupied the lower floor of the family home

Le IXe me jour

Marguerite fiele de
Abraham Bourgeois et de
Guilemette Garnier sa femme
le parin Nicolas Bertray
la marine Marguerite
Coutuere femme de Nicolas
Garnier

Le mesme jour

Extract of baptismal record of Marguerite Bourgeoys from the register
of Saint-Jean-au-Marché Church, Troyes.

that stood close by the parish church. He also held a position in the Troyes mint. Her mother came from a family involved in the production of textiles. All members of the family played an active role in the economic life of the class into which Marguerite was born. Girls as well as boys frequently learned not only the skills required for the practice of their various crafts but also the reading, writing and accounting necessary for the operation of their small family businesses. There were books in the home in which Marguerite grew up, among them the classic *Les Fleurs des vies des saints* from which she could have learned both theology and church history.

When, in later years, Marguerite described Mary's parents, she wrote of "parents who observed the law and the commandments of God and were of good repute among men." She might well have been describing her own parents. She was later to urge the sisters in her community to live always in the presence of God "as a mother who loves her child intensely does not lose him from her sight." This was something she would have learned first from watching her own mother, Guillemette, caring for her younger brothers and sisters. One of her very rare anecdotes relating to her early years illustrates how, for her, her father modelled the greatest of all God's commandments, the commandment of love, and how she grew up in a home where there was love and laughter.

Marguerite told the story many years later to try to show how important in God's eyes are even small things done out of love. She writes that they reminded her "of a present I gave my father, so small and trivial that it made those who saw it laugh, and my father as well." But, she says, "seeing that I had made it with such love, he wore it and showed it to everyone." Then she continues, "Our loving God is pleased with little virtues practised for love of him and He ennobles them in the measure that they are exercised with greater love." If Marguerite was to retain confidence in the one she called "our kind God" in the midst of all the trials of her later years, if she was to direct so much time, attention and energy toward the building of strong and loving families in New France, surely the roots lie here in the relationship between a small girl and her father.

"I was very frivolous"

Of course, all was not idyllic in the Bourgeoys household as Marguerite was growing up. Her family, too, must have been touched by the economic difficulties of the time and by the effects of war: Champagne was particularly ravaged by the Thirty Years War in the mid-1630s. Certainly the family was deeply affected by one characteristic of the time: the recurrence of epidemics that carried off large numbers of the population. Then, as is still the case, the old and the very young were particularly at risk. Of the six children born into the Bourgeoys family after Marguerite, the three who immediately followed her all died in childhood. Nevertheless, Marguerite has painted a portrait of herself as a light-hearted girl who, like many another adolescent, enjoyed spending time with a circle of friends among whom she was very popular and did not want to be thought too pious. She liked pretty clothes and jewellery, something scarcely surprising given the craft of her mother's family.

Then, in December 1638, when Marguerite was some months short of her nineteenth birthday, the life of the Bourgeoys family was irrevocably changed. Guillemette Garnier who had been well enough to take up the collection in the parish church on the first Sunday of Advent died sometime in the days immediately before Christmas. The suddenness of this death must have made it all the more shocking to her family. Guillemette was just forty-five years old. Her older children were grown: Claude and Sirette, the two eldest, were both married and had already started their families. But she left behind three young children, Édouard, aged barely ten, Madeleine, aged five and the youngest, Pierre, not yet two years old. Marguerite was not the oldest of the girls still at home. Anne and

Marie were still unmarried, but she must have been called on to help console her father and take care of the little ones. Later events would give evidence of her special affection for Madeleine and Pierre.

October 7, 1640

When Marguerite Bourgeoys left her home to take part in the Rosary procession which was part of the seasonal devotional life of her city, she had no idea that before she returned her life would have changed forever. She had reached the age of twenty and the time was coming to make a decision about how she would spend her adult life, most likely, to accept a marriage partner. Troyes can still enjoy warm golden days in early October and the size of the crowd in which she found herself that Sunday would suggest that this was one of them. She has told us that the numbers who came to participate in the event were so great that the procession was forced to move out of the Dominican monastery in which it had begun. The new route took the participants past the ancient Benedictine Abbey of Notre-Dame-aux-Nonnains. Marguerite knew what she would see along the way: her words imply that she looked up to catch a glimpse of a statue with which she was already familiar.

In spite of her description of her young self as somewhat giddy or frivolous, she was praying the rosary at that moment. Marguerite was already drawn by beauty: even her taste for adorning herself had its origin in an attraction to loveliness. But now it was another kind of beauty that she perceived as never before: the beauty of God shining through in Mary whom she was later to describe as "living water, crystal clear, springing up from the fountains of the Saviour and refreshing all who come to it." Her experience at that moment was one for which Marguerite could find no words except, "I was completely moved and changed." Her life would testify to the authenticity and depth of the experience.

Marguerite's account is filled with perhaps unconscious symbolism. This young woman who was to play so large a role in founding a new kind of religious life for women was inspired by a work of art commissioned by women who had established an earlier form of religious life in the Church. It was not just the cloister of the Dominican church that had become too small, but cloistered life itself, as God inspired new forms of religious life to meet new times. The young Marguerite was transformed by an experience of grace, not in seclusion but in the midst of a crowd. None of this, of course, was clear at the time. All that she knew was that at this moment she had given herself to God.

"The Carmelites refused me"

Marguerite wrote that when she returned home after the procession the change in her was apparent to everyone. For one thing, she gave up her pretty clothes and her more frivolous pursuits. It is easy to imagine the remarks and the teasing this must have elicited from her family and friends. Many of them must have expected that this was a passing phase and that the old Marguerite would re-emerge before long. They were wrong.

After making a general confession, she looked for a concrete way in which to give her life to God. She became part of an extern group attached to the Congrégation de Notre-Dame of Troyes whose prefect put her in touch with a priest called Antoine Gendret, chaplain to a convent of Carmelite nuns. He became her spiritual director and turned her thoughts toward religious life.

Her first inclination was toward a contemplative community, to devote her life to prayer and penance. The community to which she was especially attracted was the Carmelites and, accordingly, she applied to enter the Carmel in the Croncel district of her native city. Carmel was highly regarded in the France of Marguerite's time and was the community chosen by many members of the aristocracy and the upper middle class. Like all the religious communities in those days, it required the payment of a dowry intended to support the sister during her lifetime. Marguerite's father began to consider how to raise such a dowry, expected to be higher than the sum he would have settled on her should she have married. He did this because "he could refuse her nothing," we are told. "The Carmelites refused me even though I was strongly drawn to them," Marguerite wrote and she adds, "I went to others but this did not succeed either."

It is difficult to understand why Marguerite was refused by the Carmelites and by at least one other cloistered community. It has been suggested that perhaps her "conversion" was seen as being too sudden and too recent, but it was scarcely a conversion from a life of scandal. It has also been suggested that she might not have been seen as socially acceptable in so fashionable a community, but there were other members of her class in the Carmel of Croncels, including one of her cousins. Perhaps a more likely explanation is that the superior of Carmel, reputedly a woman of great wisdom and holiness, discerned in Marguerite another vocation. It is even possible that Father Gendret who was, after all, the chaplain of the Carmel at Croncels already had seen in her the calling to a new and very different form of religious life. But Marguerite did not know that yet and her puzzlement and disappointment were very real. Yet when she remembered these days later, she remembered not sadness or confusion but a time of feeling overwhelmed with love and joy. She was not then, nor ever would be, one to repine. If she could not give her life to God in the cloister, she would find other ways of making her gift a reality.

"I entered the Congregation where I was very faithful"

The sisters of the Congrégation de Notre-Dame founded by Alix Le Clerc and Pierre Fourier had been established in Troyes since 1628. It is possible that Marguerite attended their school; certainly, she was known to them. They were a teaching community founded in Lorraine in 1598 and had been obliged to accept the cloister in order to obtain ecclesiastical approval. A resourceful group of women, they had found a way of circumventing the barrier raised by the cloister between them and the poorer children in the outlying areas of the city. They created a group known as the extern congregation. It consisted of young women who, while they continued to live in their own homes, met at the convent and were formed and organized to teach the children who could not come to the convent themselves. Many members of this group would, of course, have been former pupils of the convent school.

Among the obligations they accepted was that of dressing simply and modestly, avoiding the "frills and furbelows" once so dear to Marguerite. She had already been invited to join the group but had declined the invitation not wanting, she said, to be thought a "bigot" and perhaps not wanting to adopt the dress code. Marguerite Bourgeoys was never an admirer of ostentatious piety, but now she was able to look beyond a surface that had somewhat repelled her to the genuine good being done by the group among the poor of Troyes. She was to remain a member of the extern congregation for thirteen years and her experiences there were to mark her for life.

A time to learn

Marguerite was to see this time in her life as a period of preparation for her mission in New France. Many of her later attitudes and practices, as well as the opinions expressed in her writings, clearly show the influence of her association with the Congrégation de Notre-Dame of Troyes. Almost from the moment of his ordination to the priesthood, Pierre Fourier had begun working to alleviate the lot of the poor in his parish. He started with almsgiving but very soon became convinced of the urgency of educating the poor so as to enable them to earn an honourable living and so remove their need to depend on alms. When Fourier founded a community of teaching sisters with Alix Le Clerc, the hope was that these could remain uncloistered or possibly could have two types of house, one cloistered and the other uncloistered.

The time had not yet come when it was possible to persuade the ecclesiastical authorities to accept this idea, but that did not cause the sisters to abandon their efforts to educate the poor: hence, the extern congregation. Fourier introduced certain pedagogical practices suited to the education of the poor in numbers, among them the use of the blackboard and the division of groups of pupils into classes. More important than methodology, the constitutions of the Congrégation de Notre-Dame also embody a philosophy of education many aspects of which are strikingly apparent in the work and writings of Marguerite Bourgeoys.

An immense awareness of the dignity and demands of the work of the teacher infuses the constitutions: only the strongest and best of the nuns would have contact with the pupils. It goes without saying, of course, that the first aim of the teacher was the religious and moral education of the pupil. But Fourier also stressed the importance of imparting the knowledge and skills needed to earn a living. In fact, although the learning of reading and writing was important,

Fourier advised that, if the poor pupil did not have the time or ability to learn these, the other skills should come first.

The constitutions stress the importance of educating women. The little girls who come to school are already an important part of the church and on them depends the future of the family, the church and, indeed, the whole of society. The school must be a place to which the children want to come. They must always be treated with respect and gentleness. Every one of these things finds an echo in Marguerite, especially in passages like this reflection on teaching:

> It is the work [most] suited to draw down the graces of God if it is done with purity of intention, without distinction between the poor and the rich, between relatives and friends and strangers, between the pretty and the ugly, between the gentle and the grumblers, looking on them all as drops of Our Lord's blood. When we must correct, we must be very moderate and act in the presence of God.

Both Alix Le Clerc and Marguerite Bourgeoys display changing attitudes toward children in some circles of the France of their time, a change that reflected and was reflected in a growing devotion to the Child Jesus. Both women were profoundly influenced by the images before which they prayed; both described mystical experiences that identified the children they taught with Christ.

Her experiences in the extern congregation must also have given Marguerite a new first-hand knowledge of poverty and its effects. The number of beggars in the area swelled as a result of the devastation caused in the surrounding countryside and the city passed laws to attempt to control the beggars already there, to prevent the entrance of beggars from outside and to control the crime associated with their presence and situation. Harsh penalties could be invoked both against the beggars and against those who aided them unlawfully. In moving about in the poorer sections of the city, Marguerite would also have been much exposed to disease. Not surprisingly, her family worried about the dangers she faced and it says much for her powers of persuasion that she was able to alleviate their worries sufficiently to allow her to continue her work. In learning to move safely and successfully among those who were scarcely among the most law-abiding or refined members of society, she was acquiring yet another ability. It would stand her in good stead in the rough inns and on the crowded ships she would experience in her travels.

Detail of a Stained-glass windows depicting the Visitation.
Saint-Rémi Church, Troyes, 16th century. Photo: Rachel Gaudreau

"The life of the journeying Virgin Mary"

In these years, Marguerite was not just involved with her work in the extern congregation. In the early 1640s, a great dream began to take shape in her life. Father Gendret continued as her spiritual director and, now that she had put aside the hope for Carmel and the cloister, he began to talk to her of another kind of religious life for women. Marguerite wrote:

> He told me one day that Our Lord had left three states of women to follow Him and to serve the Church: the role of Magdalen was filled by the Carmelites and other recluses; that of Martha, by cloistered religious who serve their neighbour; but the state of life of the journeying Virgin Mary, which must also be honoured, was not yet filled. Even without veil or wimple one could be a true religious.

In the course of her life, this vision of the role of Mary in the early Church would take clearer and clearer form for Marguerite. She saw Mary as not only the mother but also the first disciple of Jesus. Even before his birth, Mary carried him through the hill country of Judaea to visit her cousin Elizabeth and to make the unborn John the Baptist leap with joy. She sustained the Church when the Apostles fled at the time of the crucifixion. She was united in prayer with them and with the other women disciples at Pentecost and she and these other women were active in the early Church, building up Christ's mystical body as once she had given life to his physical body.

In the attempt to bring the new community into being, Marguerite was joined by two other young women. Almost certainly, they were fellow members of the extern congregation of which Louise de Chomedey, Sister Louise de Sainte-Marie, was in charge. The new little community found accommodation through another member of the Chomedey family, Jacqueline, Madame de Chevilly. This was in the Hôtel du Chaudron, close to the cathedral. Father Gendret drew up a Rule for the group and had it approved in Paris by the theologians of the Sorbonne. But Marguerite had to accept another disappointment: one of her companions got married and another died. Although this first attempt to establish a new community did not last, Father Gendret allowed Marguerite to take the step of making private vows: "I gave myself to God in 1640. A few years later [1643], upon the advice of my confessor, I took the vow of chastity, and some time later, the vow of poverty." She added that she had made these vows with all the ardour of her young heart and with the resolution of keeping them forever: "I have never had a thought contrary to this."

"They spoke to me of Canada"

Marguerite was to become intensely aware that the touch of grace that transformed her life had coincided with another event whose significance she was gradually to come to appreciate, the founding of Ville-Marie. She was to see these two events as inextricably connected and in both of them she would see the hand of God. She wrote:

> During the procession on Rosary Sunday, in the year 1640 (which I have since learned was the year of the first arrival in Montreal), I was strongly moved when I looked up at a statue of the Blessed Virgin. At the same time, M. de Maisonneuve's sister, who was a religious of the Congrégation de Notre-Dame in Troyes, gave her brother a picture on which was written in letters of gold, 'Holy Mother of God, pure Virgin with a faithful heart, keep us a place in your Montreal.

Not just here but whenever she refers to one of these events in her writings, her touch of grace or the founding of Montreal, the other immediately comes to her mind.

The France of Marguerite's time was engaged in a great movement of Catholic renewal. Although it placed special emphasis on the reform and education of the clergy, it was a movement that greatly influenced and was greatly influenced by devout members of the laity. It found inspiration in the primitive Christian Church described in the Acts of the Apostles and, like that Church, it was a missionary Church. One of the ways in which this desire to share the faith had manifested itself was in the founding of Ville-Marie on the island of Montreal in New France to carry the Christian faith to the Native Peoples of the New World. The Jesuit missionaries working in the New World were circulating written accounts of their experiences in the Jesuit Relations. Two of those in whom they awakened not only a strong response but also a will to take concrete action were Jérôme Le Royer de la Dauversière and Jean-Jacques Olier.

Jérôme Le Royer was a layman, a married man and the father of a family; his profession was that of tax collector. Even before his interest in the Montreal project, he had founded a community of nursing nuns to care for the sick in his native La Flèche. Jean-Jacques Olier was a young secular priest. Both had been educated by the Jesuits. Both belonged to the Compagnie du Saint-Sacrement, a religious association with a very large and various membership. The aim of the association was to "promote the glory of God in doing all the good to be considered true good ... and preventing all the evil to be considered true evil." Le Royer and Olier were joined by Pierre Chevrier, baron de Fancamp in organizing the Société de Notre-Dame de Montréal whose purpose was the conversion of the Native Peoples to Christianity.

The society was made up of both men and women and, although some of the members were clerics, the majority were lay people. They were inspired by the conviction that they must carry the faith to the Native Peoples of the New World, just as in the early centuries of Christianity missionaries had left the Mediterranean world to carry that faith to the rest of Europe. To realize their aim, they decided to found a settlement in New France that would be a model of a Christian society. The place they chose for its foundation was the island of Montreal whose position at the confluence of the Saint Lawrence and Ottawa rivers seemed to make it ideal as a centre for missionary activity.

Recruits were found to go to New France to make the actual foundation but the question of leadership was crucial. Finally after much prayer, the Society was able to make the choice of two people, a man and a woman both from Champagne: Paul de Chomedey de Maisonneuve, a young soldier, and Jeanne Mance who would act as bursar of the expedition, care for the sick and eventually found a hospital. In 1641, the party left France on two ships, each under the auspices of one of the two leaders. After wintering in Quebec, they sailed up the Saint Lawrence River in May 1642 to found Ville-Marie on the island of Montreal.

It was, of course, anticipated that the settlement would eventually require a school. The sisters of the Congrégation de Notre-Dame of Troyes, aware of the plans through Sister Louise, Maisonneuve's sister, hoped that they would be the ones to establish a school as the Ursulines had just done at Quebec. At the moment, all they could do was send a banner asking Our Lady to keep a place for them. They accepted that the foundation could not be made at once: thirty-one years had passed between the founding of Quebec and the arrival of the Ursulines. But they hoped that the delay would not be so long.

When Maisonneuve returned to France looking for recruits in 1652 and came to visit his sister in Troyes, the nuns begged to accompany him back to Montreal. But they were told that conditions in the new settlement were so grim that the possibility of opening a convent of cloistered nuns still lay in the unforeseeable future. They were disappointed but found hope in persuading Maisonneuve to take in their stead one lay teacher, Marguerite Bourgeoys.

A difficult decision

More than twelve years had now passed since the touch of grace that inspired Marguerite with the desire to give herself to God. By 1652, she no longer had immediate family obligations. Even her youngest brother was now fifteen years old, an adult by the standards of the time. Her much-loved father had died in October 1651. "I had the consolation of caring for him in his last illness and of burying him after his death," she wrote. But she did have other commitments: Marguerite was prefect of the extern congregation and under her leadership its numbers had grown to four hundred. There can be no doubt that there was still plenty of work to occupy her in Troyes. Also, leaving alone for a sparsely populated settlement across the world would seem to put an end to any idea of becoming part of a new kind of religious community. Marguerite was always deeply aware that her actions had consequences for others as well as herself. In this case, her local church would be affected by her choice so, before reaching a decision, she sought advice.

She turned, she tells us, to the diocesan theologian and to the representative of her bishop since the bishop himself was absent at the time. They confirmed her in the decision to go to Montreal. She turned also to her spiritual director with her misgivings. Was it wise to depart alone with Maisonneuve? What was to become of the idea of a community of women that would imitate the life of Mary? The answers she has recorded are an indication of Father Gendret's confidence in Maisonneuve, in Marguerite and, above all, in God:

> When the time came to go to Canada, my confessor told me that what God had not willed [in Troyes] he would perhaps bring to pass in Montreal ... I told him that I would be alone and that that would not be a community. He told me that I myself, my good angel and his would make a community. To this I replied that I was not being permitted to bring a companion and that I would have to go with a gentleman that I had never seen. He told me to put myself in M. de Maisonneuve's care as though I were in the care of one of the first Knights of the Chamber of the Queen of Angels. He told me that I ought to go.

Of course, she also prayed and, finally, Marguerite received a reassurance in whose light she would walk for the rest of her life:

> One morning, when I was fully awake, a tall woman dressed in a robe of white serge said to me very clearly: "Go, I will never forsake you." I knew that it was the Blessed Virgin. This gave me great courage and I found nothing difficult, even thought I feared illusions. This made me believe that if this was from God, I did not have to make any preparations for it; consequently I did not bring a penny for the journey.

Departure

In February 1653, Marguerite began the first stage of her journey toward the New World. Nowhere does she mention as reasons for her hesitation the immense hardships and dangers she was to face. Even the journey across France was fraught with difficulty as her account of it shows. The countryside through which she travelled had been devastated for the previous five years by the civil war known as the Fronde. Crossing the Atlantic on a sailing ship at the mercy of wind, weather and disease could take several months. What one would face on arrival might be even worse: reports on the severity of the Canadian winter and the torment of the mosquitoes were in common circulation in France. Above all, there was the peril of torture and death at the hands of the Iroquois. The thought of the dangers she would face must have caused considerable misgivings in the minds of those she left behind.

Marguerite set out for Paris by coach accompanied by Blaise Cossard, her maternal uncle, and by Maisonneuve's sister Jacqueline. Neither of them knew what her intentions were until the journey was underway. Their reaction to the news she gave them in the carriage is an indication of the startling nature of the step she was to take as well as the fact that she had not become a stranger to laughter in the past thirteen years: "Both he and Madame de Chevilly thought I was joking." There would, however, soon be little cause for laughter even on this first and easier stage of the journey:

On the trip from Troyes to Paris, it was Sunday and the bells were ringing for Mass. We asked the coach driver to allow us to hear Mass, but we could not obtain our request. Around noon, one of his wheels broke into two pieces. We were fifteen or sixteen. It was necessary to go to Paris for another wheel ... After dinner, a little bell rang, and a priest who appeared totally debilitated chanted Vespers with five or six sickly men. This priest told us about all the calamities of war in this place: all the houses ruined, a large number of dead horses, and even [the corpses] of some men and a woman. We tried to cover them over with a little earth.

In Paris, where Marguerite stayed with a cousin of Jeanne Mance, her resolution was tested by another kind of trial. In some quarters, there was intense hostility to the whole Montreal project, deemed by its critics and enemies to be a "crazy adventure." Attempts were made to discourage Marguerite by casting doubt on the character of Maisonneuve. Even more troubling, she was now told by the Carmelite provincial superior who was her hostess's brother that she could have a place in any Carmelite convent she chose. Once more she sought advice, this time from a Jesuit who had already served on the Canadian mission and, in fact, had contributed to the accounts that had awakened interest in that mission in France. He, too, supported her in the decision to go. But there were still obstacles to overcome.

The journey from Paris to Nantes posed other challenges than those encountered between Troyes and Paris, for Marguerite no longer had the protection of her uncle and so was exposed to all the suspicions that existed in those days about a woman travelling alone. In her later account of the trip she did not dwell on the slights she received but remembered each small kindness. She lost neither her resourcefulness nor her sense of humour as the following anecdote illustrates. When she was refused accommodation at one of the inns, a cart driver, recognizing her accent, stepped forward saying that he was from the same region and offering to pay for her room. She writes:

I was led to a room that was very far away. I closed the door and barricaded it with everything I could find. I lay down on the bed fully dressed. After some time there was a knock at the door. Someone tried to open it. Someone called out: "Countrywoman, open the door for me." After all these persistent demands, I went to the door to see whether it was really he and I spoke to him as if I were a person of great importance; I said I would bring charges against him and that I would know quite well how to have him found. Finally he went away. I heard a great deal of noise around that room. Next morning, I lifted one of the hangings and there was an open door and there was a whole crew of men, lying there asleep after having spent the whole night carousing.

She then finds an excuse for what she has seen and undergone: "These people had been hardened by war."

There was one last trial of her vocation to Canada. A Carmelite confessor "gave me scruples" about not entering Carmel, she said. Pressure about this was also put on Maisonneuve. Depressed and troubled, Marguerite went to pray in a Capuchin chapel where the Blessed Sacrament was exposed for adoration. There, "all my distress was changed and I returned with great assurance that I must go to Canada." Her commitment to Canada would never waver again.

Before boarding the ship, Marguerite was entrusted with the care of a young girl named Marie Dumesnil, an orphan on her way to Montreal in the hope of finding a husband there and starting a family. She was the first in a long line of young woman whom Marguerite would help get established in the New World and, perhaps for that reason, especially dear to Marguerite. They were joined on the voyage by a few other women and about one hundred men. The situation in the little settlement of Ville-Marie had been so precarious at his departure that Maisonneuve had come to France knowing that unless he could raise a significant recruitment the whole Montreal project would have to be abandoned. The group with which he was returning was to become known as "the great recruitment" and 1653 as the year of the second founding of Montreal.

The first ocean voyage

They did not have a smooth and easy journey. About 350 leagues (875 miles) from shore, they discovered that the ship, the Saint-Nicolas de Nantes, was leaking so much that they had to return to France and were saved from drowning only through the good offices of the people of Saint-Nazaire. By now the men recruited for Montreal were so terrified, "huddled together and trying to escape", that Maisonneuve had to keep them on an offshore island to prevent them from deserting while the ship was repaired.

After the re-launch on July 20, feast of Saint Margaret, disease broke out aboard ship. Since there was no priest on the voyage, Marguerite found herself

Drawing by S. Sainte-Marthe-de-Béthanie, around 1940.

not only caring for the sick but preparing some of them for death. By the time the Saint-Nicolas docked in Quebec, eight of the men had died and their bodies had been consigned to the ocean. How great must have been the relief when, more than three months after the first departure and after more than two months at sea, the survivors at last saw the cliffs of Quebec and were finally able to disembark on September 22, feast of Saint Maurice, though not without a further mishap. Quite literally this group of arriving immigrants burned their boat behind them. The Saint-Nicolas became stuck on a sandbar and, as it could not be dislodged, it had to be burned. Marguerite says that in the course of the journey the survivors had been changed "like clothes in the laundry."

New friendships

In spite of all the difficulties, there was also time for the growth of friendship on the voyage, friendship between Marguerite and the members of the Montreal recruitment and also between Marguerite and Maisonneuve as they discovered that they shared both values and a sense of humour. Marguerite had charge of articles of luggage given to Maisonneuve by his sister. Attempting to wash some elegant lace, she lost it in the water. His reaction when he was told about the loss was to laugh and to remark that now it would be one less thing to worry about. In the letter her wrote to Jeanne Mance announcing Marguerite's arrival, he describes her in the highest possible terms, praising both her virtue and her intelligence and assuring Jeanne that their fellow Champenoise will be a true asset to their work in Montreal.

Jeanne was in Quebec desperate for news of Maisonneuve who had now been absent for almost two years. The outlook for Montreal was so gloomy that several of the Montreal settlers had come with her, intent on giving up and returning to France. Their loss would further deplete the tiny Montreal population. The new arrivals would now more than triple that population. Jeanne's relief was at least equal to that of the settlers whose arrival, Marguerite says, "restored everyone's joy." So began a close association and friendship between Jeanne Mance and Marguerite Bourgeoys that would end only with Jeanne's death.

Maisonneuve and Jeanne Mance left at once for Montreal with the members of the recruitment well enough to continue their journey up the Saint Lawrence River; Marguerite remained at Quebec caring for those still too ill to travel. She had been invited to stay at the Ursuline convent in the Upper Town: "The Ursulines were kind enough to offer me lodging," she says, "but that was not what

I wanted." Instead, she remained with the ordinary members of the recruitment who stayed in the shed by the river that belonged to the Montreal company. Although always grateful for every act of kindness directed toward her, Marguerite would try, as far as she was able, to take her place among the ordinary people and to avoid any kind of preferential treatment. Nor did she consider her stay in the shed a penance. The men, she notes, "were as gentle as true monks. And this gave me great joy in going to Montreal." The genuine respect and liking Marguerite felt for those among whom she worked and the delight she took in them must have given them hope and confidence. The sense of solidarity she established with these future Montrealers would last throughout her life.

First fruits

The founders of 1642 had made their journey up the Saint Lawrence and first set eyes on the island of Montreal in the month of May, one of the loveliest times of year in the Saint Lawrence Valley. They had celebrated their first Mass out of doors in a meadow filled with hope and flowers and birdsong. Marguerite and her group arrived in the middle of a bleak November at a settlement where the constant danger of attack had forced even those who had begun to build outside to take refuge in the fort. She would live in that fort for more than four years.

Those years would once more demand of Marguerite an immense patience and trust and a capacity to "wait on God." This is perhaps all the more extraordinary when one remembers the precariousness of life at that time and the age she had already attained at the time of her arrival in Canada. Certainly there could as yet be no question of opening a school. There were very few women in the population and, consequently, few children. The men had to establish themselves before they could think about taking on the responsibility of a wife and family. Several of the first children born did not survive. Marguerite says that for about eight years no children survived, then, surprisingly, "This gave us great hope because God was taking the first fruits." Apparently immediately after her arrival, Marguerite was given the care of the four-and-a-half year old Jeanne Loysel, born in July 1649, and the first child to survive in Ville-Marie.

During these years Marguerite looked after the organization of Maisonneuve's household. She visited the few women already in Ville-Marie and taught them to read and write. She acted as sacristan for Father Pijart, the Jesuit who looked after the Montreal mission. She offered Jeanne Mance help at the hospital. If she ever questioned the wisdom of the decision she had made to leave her busy life in bustling Troyes to come to this remote outpost, there is no evidence of it in her writings. In fact, one of the experiences that confirmed her in the conviction that she had at last found her own true place came to her at this time.

The cross on the mountain

On their arrival in 1642, the founders of Ville-Marie had chosen a site on the banks of the Saint Lawrence where they had erected a fort in which they would spend their first winter. Unfortunately, the spot they had chosen was vulnerable to flooding and as winter approached and the waters rose higher and higher so did their fear that they were about to lose the only shelter they had. Their response was to pray that if God really intended their missionary project then God would cause the flood waters to recede. Maisonneuve promised that if they were saved they would erect a cross on Mount Royal. Their relief and joy were great when on Christmas Eve the waters began to recede. The date they chose for the fulfilment of their promise was January 6, the feast of the Epiphany, when the arrival of the Magi signalled Christ's manifestation to the nations.

Maisonneuve himself led a religious procession up the mountain, carrying the heavy piece of wood that would form the main part of the cross. Others carried

Stone tower in the grounds of the Grand Séminaire on Sherbrooke Street in Montreal. All that now remains of the Mountain Mission established by the Sulpicians in 1676 is two stone towers that were part of the fortifications erected in the 1680s. The sisters of the Congregation taught in one of these and lived in the other. Photo: Abla Mansour, Les Prêtres de Saint-Sulpice de Montréal

wood for the pedestal. Apparently Maisonneuve also took with them and left at the site the banner given him by his sister Louise and the sisters of the Congrégation de Notre-Dame of Troyes. An altar was built and the site became a place of pilgrimage where Montrealers could go to pray that the Native Peoples would be drawn to accept Christianity. Marguerite was to see in the establishment of the Mountain Mission at this site more than thirty years later the result of the prayers offered at this time by persons who would not live to see the results.

Maisonneuve himself had told Marguerite the story of the cross and promised that she would visit it. Soon after she reached Montreal, he detailed thirty men to take her to the site. The struggles over the fur trade and the rivalry between the Iroquois and the Native allies of the French had not made the ensuing years a very favourable time for evangelization and, by the time of Marguerite's arrival, the cross on the mountain had been overturned by the Iroquois. The cross was important enough to these first Montrealers that they decided to re-erect it and Marguerite was given the task of supervising the work. She took with her Gilbert Barbier, the carpenter, and several other men, and the group spent three consecutive days working on the project.

Now occurred one of the great moments of mystical awareness that mark the life of Marguerite Bourgeoys and, like the touch of grace in 1640, it happened not in seclusion but at a moment when she was closely involved with other people. In spite of all the depredations that had taken place at the site, she found the banner given to Maisonneuve by his sister before his departure from France. It was badly damaged but she could still read the inscription: "Holy Mother of God, pure Virgin with a royal heart, keep us a place in your Montreal." Marguerite's several references to this discovery in her writings indicate how very important this find was in her life. For the first time, she associated her touch of grace in 1640 with the founding of Montreal and each time she mentions the banner afterwards, it is to connect the two events. She now came to the certain conviction that during the past thirteen years God had been preparing her for her vocation in Montreal. Although she had arrived so recently, it was as though she had been there all along and the place Mary had been saving was for her.

A new place of pilgrimage

But these were difficult days in the little settlement and almost at once it became much too dangerous for pilgrims to make their way up the mountain to the cross. Yet this deprived the settlers of what was an important form of prayer at the time. The plan of the founders of Ville-Marie was that there would be a parish church dedicated to Mary, but that would not be built in the foreseeable future. These two facts prompted Marguerite to undertake in 1655 what might have seemed another "crazy adventure", the building of a chapel of pilgrimage dedicated to the Blessed Virgin. It is a "crazy adventure" whose result has endured to this day.

The way in which Marguerite went about it shows some of her organizing ability and capacity to inspire others to work together. She chose a site on the banks of the Saint Lawrence east of the fort, close enough that pilgrims could visit it in safety. She approached and involved the proper authorities. Father

Pijart gave his permission for the building of the chapel and chose its name: Notre-Dame de Bon-Secours, Our Lady of Good Help. This must have pleased Marguerite who tells us that she always counted on the help of the Blessed Virgin. Too, it gave the settlers a patron to whom they could turn in hope during these truly perilous times. Another Jesuit missionary, Simon Le Moyne, laid the first stone. Maisonneuve had wood cut for the framework and he himself helped drag the logs in from the woods and had the timbers squared. Marguerite invited anyone who was able to help to gather stones for what would be a fieldstone building. She collected alms to pay the masons. Other workers prepared the lime, the sand and the boards and, in some cases, she offered to sew for them in exchange for a day's work. Eventually she had collected enough material to build and roof the chapel and

Virtual historical representation of the first chapel of Notre-Dame-de-Bon-Secours. Omar Bakat, GRAPH Architecture Inc.

the foundations had been laid. Then came a setback: a change in ecclesiastical jurisdiction in Montreal resulted in a suspension of the work. Marguerite once more had the opportunity to practise both patience and perseverance.

Arrival of the Sulpicians

Jean-Jacques Olier was not only one of the founding members of the Montreal Society. He was also the founder of an association of priests known now as the Priests of Saint Sulpice, named after the church in Paris where the association began. The purpose of the Jesuits in coming to New France had been the mission to the First Nations rather than the spiritual care of the European settlers. Their numbers had been depleted by the martyrdom between 1642 and 1649 of six Jesuit priests and two lay workers. They had, therefore, for some time, hoped to find other priests to take over their work in Ville-Marie.

In 1655, the signing of a temporary peace with the Iroquois had permitted Maisonneuve to return to France once more and there to arrange that the Sulpicians would assume pastoral responsibility for Ville-Marie. He returned in 1657 with four of them. The superior, Gabriel Thubières de Levy de Queylus, was soon caught up in disputes about the administration of the Church in Canada and so had little time for Montreal. He believed the building of the chapel of pilgrimage should be at least postponed.

It was, in fact, Gabriel Souart who became the first acting parish priest of Ville-Marie and very soon a friend and supporter of Marguerite Bourgeoys. Struggles and quarrels about the administration of the Canadian Church were to continue for many years, exacerbated both by problems in the French Church and its relationship to Rome and by the convictions and personalities of the people involved in the dispute. They were to cause much grief both to the participants and to other Christians whose lives they affected.

As in any period, Marguerite had to live in charity with a Church that is never perfect or finished but always under construction. In spite of the difficulties with Abbé de Queylus, Marguerite's Congregation that would soon begin to take shape was to benefit greatly from the spiritual, moral and material support of the Sulpicians. Many of them believed in Marguerite's vision of a community of sisters whose chapel was the parish church and who were able to move freely among the people they sought to serve. That support would be an important factor in the survival of the young Congregation, both in the seventeenth century and later.

The stable school

Though Marguerite was disappointed that work on the chapel had to be suspended, she was delighted to find that the purpose for which she had come to Montreal was to be realized at last. As the settlers began to build little houses outside the fort and the number of children began to increase, it finally became possible to open a school. At the end of January 1658, Maisonneuve deeded to Marguerite Bourgeoys and her successors a stone building on the common less than half way between the fort and the site chosen for the Chapel of Notre-Dame-de-Bon-Secours. The gift and its acceptance were an act of hope on both their parts.

The building was constructed of stone and had served as a communal stable until the herdsman was killed in an Iroquois raid in 1652. It consisted of a lower area about thirty-six by eighteen feet and a dovecote above reached by a removable ladder. There was much work to be done before it would be ready to receive the children. Marguerite had a chimney and hearth installed, an amenity the previous animal inhabitants had not enjoyed, and she worked with the children to scrub the place clean and remove all traces of the former occupants.

Marguerite's involvement of the children in the preparation of their school was a useful way of finding necessary support. But it was also typical of the way in

Marguerite Bourgeoys with Ville-Marie's first school. Painting by S.S.-René (Elmina Lachance), 1904. Used in 1975 for the Canadian postage stamp commemorating the 275th anniversary of the death of Marguerite Bourgeoys.

which she worked with people. She understood that working together is an excellent means of establishing bonds between people, of forming them into a community. She also understood that participation in the creation of a project develops a sense of ownership often absent when the project is someone else's responsibility. So when the children of Montreal began their classes on April 30, 1658, feast of Saint Catherine of Siena, they did so in a school that was truly theirs.

As Marguerite took up residence in the stable school, there can be no doubt that it had a special significance for her. In a stable, Mary had given birth to Jesus. There she had received "shepherds and kings with the same love." Now Marguerite would receive in her stable school the children who were already so important a part of the Church of Montreal, of the mystical Christ, and who were certainly its hope for the future. She never lost her love for this her first real home in Montreal and the cradle of what would soon become a community of women who would try to emulate the life of Mary.

Looking to the future

In the summer of 1658, Marguerite's thoughts were not just of the present, however; already she was looking toward the future. As the number of children continued to increase, she would need companions to help with the work. At the moment, little Jeanne Loysel was still with her and a young woman called Marguerite Picard was helping her, but both of these would eventually marry, Marguerite Picard as soon as the following autumn. If Marguerite Bourgeoys' work was to continue, if it was to grow and be given stability, then dedicated and permanent companions would be necessary and these were not likely to be found in New France in the immediate future. Also, Marguerite continued to cherish the hope that somehow the community she had first dreamed of in Troyes would come to be.

The time had come to seek help in France and providentially, in her view, an opportunity presented itself. Jeanne Mance had fallen on the ice and broken her right arm more than a year before. Because the injury had not healed properly and had left her somewhat handicapped, she wanted to go to France to see if anything could be done to lessen her disability. Jeanne also had another purpose for she too was looking toward the future, aware that she was both aging and in

La facilité de vous escrire que vous m'offrites
passé me donne La liberté de vous faire savoir...
qui ont porté a faire L'establissement de la Congregatio
Montreal; et comme j'apprends que vous avez La charité
travaillez aux Reglements qui y doivent Seriz, Je passé
Repugnance pour vous faire savoir Les fins de Cet...
Monsieur Jeandret qui me voulut bien prendre sous Sa direction
un Jour, que Notre Seigneur avoit Laissé 3 etats de filles...
et Seriz L'eglise; que Celuy de Ste Madeleine etoit rempli par...
et autres Veuves, et Celuy de Ste Marthe par Les Religieuses Cloit...
Seroient Le prochain; Mais que Celuy de La vie voyagere de la...
ne Letoit pas, et quil falloit Lhonorer..... Je croys que pour honorer...
La vie voyagere de la Ste Vierge il faut que Les Soeurs soient filles...
quelles soient gouvernées par Les Seminaires, que Les derniers Sacrements...
... de la paroisse, quelles y ayent une sepulture et...

Extract of a letter written in 1695 by Marguerite Bourgeoys to Louis Tronson, Superior of the Sulpicians in Paris. In the letter she explains the origins of the Congregation. Reproduction : Archives du Musée Marguerite-Bourgeoys. Original document : Archives des Prêtres de Saint-Sulpice à Paris . (2B/01) ill health. To guarantee the continued existence of the hospital she had founded, she hoped to arrange for the coming of nursing nuns. Founded in La Flèche by Jérôme Le Royer, the Hospitalières de Saint-Joseph were the nuns whose presence in Montreal had been anticipated from the beginning. The two women made plans together. Both would go to France to look for reinforcements and Marguerite would take care of Jeanne on the journey.

Preparing for departure

Jeanne and Marguerite had first to ensure that their work would continue during an absence that would last at least a year. They had, of course, to arrange matters with Abbé de Queylus before their departure. From this rose a serious problem for Jeanne Mance. During his stay there, the Abbé had been greatly impressed by the work of the Quebec hospital sisters. It now occurred to him that Jeanne Mance's absence would provide a perfect opportunity to install that community in Montreal in place of Jeanne Mance and the hospitallers originally intended for Ville-Marie. Accordingly, he sent two of the Quebec hospital sisters up to Montreal on the pretext that the health of one of them demanded a change of air. Their arrival greatly distressed both Jeanne Mance and Maisonneuve;

however, with the help of Marguerite Bourgeoys, an acceptable solution was worked out. The two hospital sisters would take care of the stable school during her absence and one of the Montreal women would replace Jeanne Mance temporarily.

Marguerite also had another kind of problem to resolve. In early August, she had been urged to undertake the care of an Iroquois baby girl whose mother was neglecting her. Although she hesitated about the circumstances, Marguerite was finally persuaded to adopt the child who became the first Iroquois to be baptized. The baptism took place on August 5, feast of Our Lady of the Snows, and the child was given the name Marie-des-Neiges. Now Marguerite had to find someone to look after her new daughter during her absence. She confided her to the care of one of the local women who was childless. Jeanne and Marguerite left Montreal for Quebec on September 30. There they would board the ocean-going vessel that would carry them back to their native land.

The return journey to France lasted into early winter. Jeanne seems to have been troubled by the fact that there was no priest aboard the ship that was almost completely manned by Huguenots who were able to publicly profess their religion when they were at sea. The two women spent much of the voyage in the gunroom. It was, in a many ways, one of Marguerite's easier voyages: congenial companionship, absence of disease and a seemingly well-behaved crew.

But her heart must have lifted when the towers of La Rochelle came into sight. The two women spent the feast of the Epiphany at La Flèche with the hospital nuns; then Marguerite accompanied Jeanne to Paris where she left her in the care of her sister. There, Jeanne consulted doctors, among them the king's physician, but she was told that her arm had already atrophied and that nothing could be done for her. Her help was to come from a quite different source.

There is no better account of what then happened than that written by Jeanne herself. On February 2, feast of the Purification, she went to visit the church and seminary of Saint-Sulpice where she was given the special privilege of entering the private Sulpician chapel. Since her last visit to France, Jean-Jacques Olier had died. As was then the custom with persons who had been regarded as holy during their lifetime, Olier's heart had been removed after death and placed in a reliquary. Jeanne had asked to hold this reliquary not, she says, with the intention of asking for a cure but simply to venerate the relic of a man whose holiness she wished to remember and honour. Then something wholly unexpected happened:

> As I entered the chapel, I was overcome by a great rush of joy so extraordinary that in all my life I had never felt anything like it ... I cannot explain my experience except in saying that it was an effect of the great joy I felt at the happiness into which the servant of God had now entered. I spoke to him as if he were there before my eyes and with much greater confidence, certain that he now understood me much better than when he was in this world: that he saw my needs and the sincerity of my heart which had nothing hidden from him.

The sensation of joy continued throughout the Mass. When Jeanne was given the reliquary, she took it in her left hand and placed it on the injured right arm, which was bandaged up and in a sling. She could feel the weight but was free from all sense of pain as warmth flowed back into the injured limb. On February 13 she used her newly restored right arm to write an official attestation of what had happened.

Troyes once more

After leaving Jeanne with her sister in Paris, Marguerite had gone at once to Troyes. There she received in surprise and delight the letter Jeanne immediately wrote to tell her of the cure. On this return to the city of her birth, Marguerite stayed with the sisters of the Congrégation de Notre-Dame though she must also have visited members of her family still living in Troyes. Marie, the sister closest to her in age, had died during Marguerite's absence but her husband and children remained. During this return to Troyes, Marguerite formally renounced her share of her family inheritance in favour of Madeleine and Pierre, her youngest sister and brother.

In her search for companions willing to accompany her to Canada, Marguerite turned once more to the extern congregation she had led before her departure for Montreal. Catherine Crolo had been eager to accompany Marguerite even on the first voyage. Now she could finally fulfill her desire to go to Ville-Marie. Marguerite found a second recruit in Edmée Chastel whose father was an apostolic notary whom Marguerite described as "a good servant of God." Sensitive as ever to the thoughts and feelings of others, Marguerite was aware of his concern for a deeply loved daughter. When he asked how the group would live in

Montreal, Marguerite showed him the contract for the stable school and assured him that she could provide bread and soup and that they would work to earn their living. The anxious father sought the reassurance of the bishop and Edmée signed a contract engaging her to live in community and to teach both the children of the settlers and any First Nations children who presented themselves in the school. M. Chastel took other steps to ensure his daughter's future well-being: he made sure she left, not with a little bundle of absolute necessities as Marguerite herself had done, but with a well-filled trunk. He wrote to some of his contacts along the way they would travel, asking that she be given everything she might need if she wished to return to Troyes. As a final piece of insurance, he had her sew 150 *livres* in gold coins into her clothing. Edmée showed no such hesitation but gave up her property in favour of her godchildren. Like Marguerite herself, both Catherine and Edmée were in their late thirties at this time.

Marie Raisin, the third recruit from Troyes, was just twenty-three years old. Her father, a prosperous master tailor, now lived in Paris where his other child, a son, was a lawyer in the parlement. He was, at first, extremely reluctant to let his only daughter leave for the dangers and privations of the New World and it was only after many tears and much pleading on her part that he finally gave his consent. The fourth recruit, Anne Hioux, also in her early twenties, joined the group in Paris. After the usual difficulties involved in travel at that time, the group reached La Rochelle where they met Jeanne Mance and the three hospital nuns who were to work at the Hôtel-Dieu in Montreal.

The voyage on the Saint-André

The ship embarked on July 2, feast of the Visitation of Mary to her cousin Elizabeth. This time there were priests aboard, two Sulpicians on their way to Montreal. Jeanne Mance shared a cabin with the hospital nuns. Marguerite and her companions shared a common cabin with a group of about eighteen women on their way to New France in the hope of marrying and establishing families. There were also several other women and families.

For Marguerite, this was the moment in which her Congregation was born, the moment when its members, like Mary, set off to carry Christ wherever they might be needed. They lived in community together for the first time. As was fitting, they did so among the people they hoped to serve, not as a group set apart. Their confidence and resolve were to be much tested in the course of the voyage.

Unknown to its passengers before their departure, the Saint-André had previously been used by the army as a hospital ship. As a consequence, disease soon broke out on board; everyone was sick to some extent and there were several deaths. Although she too was weakened by illness, Marguerite, we are told, worked unceasingly among the sick and the dying. The Thibaudeau family from Marans was among those severely affected. The parents and three of the four children fell ill and the youngest, just a few months old, cried incessantly. When Marguerite heard someone threaten to throw the baby overboard, she herself took over its care. This created difficulties because the crying disturbed the other women with whom she was sharing a cabin, most of whom were both sick and frightened. By the time the ship landed at Quebec, the Thibaudeau parents were somewhat recovered physically, although their three older children had all died at sea. To give some respite to the women whose quarters she shared, Marguerite returned the baby to her parents. They, however, left her too near the fire so that she suffered burns to her back. Marguerite again took the little one in charge for the trip up the river to Montreal, regretting only that she had no ointment to ease the baby's pain. Once back in Ville-Marie, she found a wet nurse to care for the baby, but the struggles of the voyage had been too much and the baby died.

Marguerite Bourgeoys with Jeanne Mance on her second voyage back to New-France.
Drawing by S.Sainte-Marthe-de-Béthanie, around 1940.

First days of the Congregation

Marguerite and her four companions reached Montreal on September 30, 1659, exactly a year after she and Jeanne Mance had begun their journey. This time, Marguerite arrived at her destination not in the bleakness before the onset of winter but amid the glories of the early autumn forest. In spite of all the difficulties encountered, this journey ended in hope and joy that at last she had companions with whom to share her life and to participate in the creation of a new kind of religious community. Amid the greeting of old friends and the introduction of new ones, she did have one disappointment: all the materials she had collected to build the chapel of pilgrimage had disappeared during her absence, no doubt gone into the construction of some settler's house.

The situation in Ville-Marie continued to be dangerous and the ladder leading to the sleeping quarters in the stable school had to be pulled in every night. The school continued to offer temporary shelter to young women who had come to Montreal to marry. It also served as a public building where marriage contracts were signed and where wakes over the deceased could be held on the eve of their burial. The school population continued to grow.

New friendships were formed. The hospital nuns, after some difficulty with the newly arrived bishop of Quebec, François de Montmorency Laval, were finally allowed to go to Montreal in November and between the two communities began a friendship that would continue for centuries. The hospital nuns received their first Canadian candidate, Marie Morin, who came from Quebec to join them in 1662, and Marguerite and her first companions formed the choir for her profession ceremony in March 1665. Sister Morin became the annalist at Montreal's Hôtel-Dieu and eventually set down her memories of this time. It is to her pen that we owe the most vivid, detailed and often moving descriptions of life in early Montreal in recollections that successfully convey not just the heroism but also the humanity of its inhabitants. Among these is the picture of Maisonneuve, Abbé Souart and Marguerite Bourgeoys encouraging one another on some of Montreal's darkest and most dangerous days in shared jokes and laughter.

For the sake of families

Events in Europe always affected life in New France despite the distance. In 1662, Louis XIV had begun his period of direct rule in France and among the policies implemented by his minister Colbert was a plan to strengthen the

French colonies in America and make them profitable. One aspect of this plan was to recruit and subsidize the settlement of women willing to come to North America to marry the colonists already established. The first such group to reach Montreal arrived in 1663. Marguerite already had experience with the initiation of young women who had been sponsored by the Montreal Society, beginning with Marie Dumesnil in 1653. Marguerite herself described the arrival of the latest newcomers: "I went to meet them at the shore, believing that we must open wide the doors of the Blessed Virgin's house to all young women." Since they still lived in the stable school, this made her companions decide that their quarters were becoming too crowded.

As usual, Marguerite treated their opinions with respect and consideration but she did not abandon the hospitality she believed she owed the new arrivals. The previous year she had bought a small house nearby. She had this put in order and moved into it with the women who became known as the *filles du roi*. She wrote, "I lived with them because this was for the establishment of new families." For the decade in which groups of these women continued to arrive, Marguerite and her companions offered them hospitality, friendship and initiation into the skills that they would need to survive the harsh conditions of their new environment.

As early as 1662, Marguerite had obtained a land grant near the river in Pointe-Saint-Charles. There she began the cultivation of a farm that would help support the work of her Congregation into the first quarter of the twentieth century. Beginning in 1668, she also had a farmhouse on the land. Catherine Crolo took charge of this and there, tradition says, she received some of the *filles du roi* who arrived after that date. It would be difficult to overestimate the importance of the support Marguerite's congregation offered to these women, most of whom were from cities and ill-prepared for the challenges they faced.

Travelling missions

Their uncloistered status not only permitted Marguerite and her companions to offer hospitality and share their home with others; it also enabled them to go out to others as the Virgin Mary had done in her visit to her cousin Elizabeth. Beginning in the early 1660s they began to undertake what were known as the travelling missions. The population of New France was very thinly spread and the number of clergy few. The problem of education in the faith was therefore serious. In this situation, the members of Marguerite's Congregation began to travel to the more remote areas to spend several weeks preparing the young people for First Communion, a rite that took place at about the age of twelve or thirteen. According to the conditions of the time, this was the threshold of adulthood: girls could marry at twelve and both boys and girls could enter into the work force at an even younger age. The instruction given by the sisters might be the only formal religious instruction their pupils would ever receive. Marguerite undertook all this in the early days with only three companions since Edmée Chastel had decided not to remain with the group. She remained in New France for the rest of her life but not as a member of the Congregation.

A changing world

The mid-1660s brought great changes to all of New France, but particularly to Montreal. Despite all that he had done to establish the missionary colony of Ville-Marie, despite the fact that he was neither incompetent nor venal, as were so many others colonial officials, Maisonneuve was recalled to France in 1665. He would remain nominal governor of Ville-Marie for several years more, but he would never return.

The same year saw the arrival of the reinforcements for which he and many of the other authorities, both civil and ecclesiastical, had been begging for so many years. The Carignan-Salières Regiment under the command of the Marquis de Tracy would bring about many changes in New France. Their presence resulted in a period of peace between the French and the Iroquois. Many of the members of the regiment chose to remain after their period of service was completed and so added significantly to the population. Their presence and the continued arrival of the *filles du roi* meant that there would be much work for Marguerite and her companions to do to assist families and to educate their children. Although she was disappointed not yet to be able to build the chapel of pilgrimage, Marguerite acceded to the wishes of her companions and began building a larger and more convenient house.

François de Montmorency Laval, Canada's first bishop, had arrived at Quebec in June 1659. The following year, he made an apostolic visit to his new diocese, beginning at Gaspé. The bishop himself, although a member of one of France's oldest families, lived in the greatest simplicity and was truly dedicated to the welfare of the poorest and most vulnerable among his people. When he reached Montreal, he was very favourably impressed both by the work being done by the Congregation and by the sisters' way of life: they too lived in the utmost simplicity, sleeping on straw mattresses and sharing the coarse bread of the ordinary colonists. Any luxuries they possessed, like sheets, were kept for the use of the poor in whom they recognized the presence of Christ.

In 1669, the bishop gave the Congregation his authorization to teach anywhere they were invited to do so in his diocese. Since this stretched from Hudson Bay to the Gulf of Mexico, he was giving them a very large commission. As Marguerite looked toward the future and the increasing need for the services of her little group, she realized that she must once more return to France, both to establish the Congregation on a more official footing and to enlist new members.

The second voyage

The extent of her foresight and practical skills is evident in the preparations Marguerite made for her journey. She collected documents testifying to the value and success of the work the Congregation was doing in the colony, including an endorsement by the citizens of Montreal passed in an assembly in 1668. She had documents drawn up indicating that any property acquired by the Congregation belonged to the group rather than to her alone. And, to make sure that the site for Notre-Dame-de-Bon-Secours Chapel would not be lost during her absence, as the materials in 1658-59 had been, she had a simple wooden structure built on it. Then she set off for what would be her longest absence from Montreal between the time of her arrival and the time of her death. Before setting sail from Quebec, Marguerite found that her box containing her precious papers and whatever else she had prepared for the journey had not been put on board. Despite her efforts to recover it, the best she could do was to make sure the papers would follow her on the next ship. This time she had with her perhaps even less than when she had sailed for New France with only her little bundle in 1653. However, she found a coil of rope to use as a bed and a piece of sailcloth to fashion into a shift. She arrived in La Rochelle in mid-autumn. The voyage had lasted only a month, she wrote.

Marguerite saw in her experiences during this her second return to her native land a powerful example of God's care for those who put all their trust in Him. She arrived in Paris with neither money nor material goods of any kind (even the sailcloth shift had somehow disappeared), but God's care reached her again and again through the kindness of others, and sometimes in very unexpected ways. She went first to the Sulpician seminary where she was referred to a nearby house at which she could spend the night. The next morning, she went to deliver a letter to the sisters of Montreal's parish priest. "They offered me breakfast," she remembered, "which I accepted, with need." On her way back to the seminary, she joined a procession following a priest carrying the Blessed Sacrament, a devotional practice of the time favoured even by the king, and stopped in a church to pray and to go to confession. Then she says that as she was waiting at the door of the seminary, she heard a priest say, "I have been told to give 100 *livres* to a woman I don't know." She continues, "When I heard him mention the name, I said, 'It's mine!' M. Perot, the younger, confirmed the truth of this. At once I followed this gentleman who lived on the *rue* Principesse. He gave me 100 *livres*. I gave him a receipt in duplicate." Both this and another sum offered to her appear to have been payment for earlier loans she had no longer expected to be paid back.

There were others to contact, the first among them, Paul de Chomedey de Maisonneuve whom she went to find the day after she reached the capital. The reunion of these two old friends was one of the events that remained vivid in her memory: "When I knocked at the door, he came down (for he lived on the third and fourth floors with Louis Frin), and opened the door to me with great joy." Maisonneuve remained deeply attached to Montreal and hungry for news of what was happening there. In the Paris lodgings he occupied with his manservant, he had prepared a special guest room for visitors from Montreal. Marguerite was the first to occupy it. There must have been much news and many memories to share, and, no doubt, some of the old laughter.

Maisonneuve added his testimonial to those that Marguerite had brought from Canada, describing her work and accomplishments and those of her companions. From this time until his death he looked after the financial affairs of the Congregation in France. The letters patent establishing the Congrégation de Notre-Dame de Montréal as a legal entity were signed by King Louis XIV at Dunkirk in May 1671.

New members for the Congregation

Marguerite could now give her attention to the other matter that had brought her to France: the recruitment of new members for the Congregation. As before, she returned to her native city where she was reunited with the members of her family and with the sisters of the Congrégation de Notre-Dame of Troyes. Her three nieces, the daughters of her sister Marie and of Orson Sommillard, decided to accompany their aunt back to Canada. Marguerite Sommillard, the oldest, had already decided to become a member of her aunt's Congregation;

Louise, the middle sister, intended to marry as, perhaps did Catherine, the youngest of the three, just sixteen years old. Bishop Laval was in France and received Marguerite Sommillard and five other women into the Congregation in the chapel of the Foreign Missions Society in Paris. After this, the group set off for the port of Le Havre to take ship for Canada.

Notre-Dame-de-Bon-Secours

By 1663, with many of its original members already dead, the Société de Notre-Dame de Montréal had almost ceased to exist. The Sulpicians had then accepted responsibility for the island with the immense debt accrued since the foundation of Ville-Marie. However, one of its most prominent and generous members, Pierre Chevrier, baron de Fancamp, still took an active and lively interest in the project in whose origins he had played so important a role. He now offered to pay for Marguerite's voyage; she asked, rather, for a gift for the chapel of pilgrimage she still hoped to build in Montreal. When she visited him on her way to the coast, he gave her a wooden statuette of the Virgin and Child, about six inches high that had been carved, perhaps more than a century earlier from an oak tree regarded as sacred, in what is now Belgium. The statuette, placed in a

Foundation of the 1678 chapel uncovered in the archaeological explorations below the present chapel in 1996-97. This photograph of the foundation of the apse shows the holes left by stakes when the wooden palisade surrounding the town was extended to take in the Faubourg Bonsecours and the apse became part of the fortifications.

Photo: Rachel Gaudreau

The present day chapel on St. Paul Street in Old Montreal was constructed in 1771 over the foundations of the first stone chapel.

Photo: Normand Rajotte

Marguerite first began to plan a chapel of pilgrimage dedicated to the Blessed Virgin in 1655. After many delays, the chapel, Montreal's first stone church, was completed in 1678 and dedicated to Notre-Dame-de-Bon-Secours. It was destroyed by fire in 1754 and the present chapel erected over the original foundations in 1771. Using information from historical documents and from recent archaeological discoveries, this computer-assisted projection pictures the chapel as it might have looked in its natural setting about 1680.

Virtual historic reconstruction:
Omar Bakat, GRAPH Architecture Inc.

Statuette of Virgin and Child in oak given to Marguerite Bourgeoys by the Baron de Fancamp in 1672 for the chapel of pilgrimage whose construction she had begun in Montreal. Already a century old at the time of its presentation, the statuette has survived both fire and theft and is now preserved in Notre-Dame-de-Bon-Secours Chapel in Montreal.

Photo: Normand Rajotte

Holy water font in glazed earthenware, one of the artifacts recovered during the archaeological excavations beneath Notre-Dame-de-Bon-Secours Chapel in 1996-97.

Photo: Pierre Fauteux, Collection of the Ministère de la culture et des communications du Québec; Ville de Montréal

Two sides of a reliquary of Marguerite Bourgeoys. It contains ashes of her heart. On the reverse side is a fragment of paper bearing the words "St gabriel" in Marguerite Bourgeoys's handwriting.

Photo: Bernard Dubois

A small box made of stillborn calfskin that belonged to Marguerite Bourgeoys and was perhaps the one containing her papers and articles that was accidentally left behind at Quebec at the beginning of her second return to France in 1670-72.

Photo: Bernard Dubois

Image showing Marguerite Bourgeoys upon her arrival at Ville-Marie with the great recruitment of 1653. At her side, Marie Dumesnil, a young girl taken under Marguerite's wing until her marriage. Painting by Rachel Gaudreau.

Photo : Normand Rajotte

Portrait of Jeanne Le Ber, the recluse of Ville-Marie. She is represented with the first chapel of Notre-Dame-de-Bon-Secours and the Old Seminary. As her regard falls serenely on her embroidery, she prays for Ville-Marie.

© Illustration by François Thisdale. Photo : Normand Rajotte

Marguerite Bourgeoys first received a land grant at Pointe-Saint-Charles in 1662. This property was added to over time, and the farm established there helped support the work of the Congregation until the first quarter of the twentieth century. It is now a museum recalling especially the work done by the Congregation with early female immigrants to Montreal.

Photos: Pierre Guzzo, Maison Saint-Gabriel

Stained-glass windows depicting events in the life of the Virgin Mary that were central to the spirituality of Marguerite Bourgeoys: Pentecost and Visitation. Saint-Rémi Church, Troyes, 16th century.

Photos: Rachel Gaudreau

Two watercolours by the illustrator Monique Chaussé showing Marguerite Bourgeoys contributing to daily chores in the young colony of Ville-Marie.

Photos: Rachel Gaudreau

Brass engraving with image of Virgin and Child described in the documents as "copper medal of the Blessed Virgin" and placed with the commemorative plaque in 1675.

Photo: Pierre Fauteux, Ville de Montréal

Lead commemorative plaque placed under the first stone of the foundation of Notre-Dame-de-Bon-Secours Chapel on 30 June 1675.

Photos: Pierre Fauteux, Ville de Montréal

jewelled reliquary, was already associated with miraculous happenings, the latest of these the recent recovery of the baron from a serious illness. Marguerite carried this safely to Canada, where to the present day it has survived the upheavals and mishaps of the intervening centuries, including theft and fire.

Return to Ville-Marie

One can only begin to imagine the relief and happiness of Marguerite's companions at receiving her home again that autumn of 1672. Marguerite once wrote that the Blessed Virgin drew others to good by her example, that just to see her was to be drawn to holiness. This seems to have been a characteristic she herself possessed in great

Painting executed by Father Savoia, O.P. in Rome for the canonization of Marguerite Bourgeoys in 1982.

measure. To have once more among them Marguerite's courage, her energy, her joy and her hope would alone have been a cause for rejoicing. But her return also brought them a new security in the form of the letters patent and new companions to share their life and their work. Fortunately, the new house was finished so that it was no longer necessary to accommodate all of them in the stable-school.

An eventful decade

The years following Marguerite's return from France were filled with new life and activity: the establishment of permanent missions outside Ville-Marie, the real beginnings of missionary work among the Native Peoples and the entry of North American women into the Congregation. It was also a time of goodbyes. Jeanne Mance had been in poor health for some time. She died in June 1673, and tradition places Marguerite Bourgeoys at her side during her final hours. Maisonneuve died in Paris in September 1676. His last will and testament drawn up on the eve of his death shows how much his beloved Montreal still occupied his thoughts and interests: the largest bequest was to Marguerite's Congregation, the next to the Hôtel-Dieu of Montreal. Marguerite Bourgeoys was now the only one left of the three from Champagne who had given so much to the little colony.

Marguerite was also involved closely with events following the death of someone whose life was neither so long nor so illustrious. Her story reveals much about the relationship of Marguerite Bourgeoys with the early colonists. On a July evening in 1673, a distraught woman named Françoise Nadereau arrived at the door of the Congregation asking to see Marguerite Bourgeoys. Although only in her late twenties at this time, Françoise had already experienced violence and loss in her life: her first husband had been killed on his own doorstop in an Indian attack. She married again, to a member of the same recruitment that had brought Marguerite to Montreal. Although the first child of this marriage died, there were by now four others and it was about the second of these that she had come.

Her daughter Catherine, five-and-a-half years old, was dead. Catherine had died by strangulation and at first the mother told Marguerite that it had happened when her daughter had tried to escape from a cupboard in the barn where her mother had placed her as punishment after she threw dirt into the eyes of her little brother. Marguerite went with the woman to report the accident, first to the religious and then to the civil authorities. But afterwards, the mother broke down and told Marguerite the true story, the story she had been too frightened to tell the authorities.

Catherine had been a mischievous child and her mother, with four children ranging from one to seven years old and all the tasks of a pioneer household to see to, had taken to putting her into a barrel to cool off when she was especially naughty. But Catherine was also resourceful and soon had learned to climb out of the barrel. She was able to do so even when her mother put planks over the opening and a sack of meal on top of the planks. She was proud of demonstrating her prowess to the neighbour's children and had done so on the morning of the day she died. She was again in the barrel in the afternoon.

When she did not appear for supper, her mother went to set her free but found her dead, caught between the rim of the barrel and the planks and unable to cry out. Marguerite helped this woman to find the witnesses she needed to corroborate her story and to clear her of the suspicion of murdering her child. In Marguerite, this frightened woman found someone in whom she could confide the mistakes she did not dare reveal to anyone else and the compassion and support she so sorely needed.

Canonical approbation

In May 1676, after an absence of four years in France, Bishop Laval arrived in Montreal to make his pastoral visit. He came to the Congregation in June and what he saw there inspired him to encourage and strengthen the group by issuing his canonical approbation of the filles séculières de la Congrégation de Notre-Dame. (The term "secular women" distinguished them from nuns, a term associated with cloister). In the document, the bishop speaks of their life in community and their work as school teachers both of religion and of the skills needed to earn a living. He stresses the fact that the teaching is offered gratis and that the sisters are self-supporting through their farm and through the work of their hands, a burden to no one. He also makes it clear that he is not approving a form of "religious life" for to him that term meant cloister and one of his strongest reasons for approving the new group was precisely their ability to travel and so to help meet the needs of his vast diocese.

The members of the Congregation could not make public vows but their form of community life was approved, at least for the moment: they could receive new members, and they could reach out to other places in their vast diocese. It may have been at this time that Catherine Sommillard, the youngest of Marguerite's nieces, was formally received into the Congregation for, like her oldest sister, she chose the Congregation rather than marriage.

The Mountain Mission

The first new place to which the sisters of the Congregation went was in fact quite close at hand and intended as a means toward the fulfilment of the purpose for which Montreal had been founded. In 1676, the Sulpicians began a mission to the Native Peoples near the place where the cross had been raised in 1643. Since the establishment of peace after 1665, a village had grown up in this area, home to both Christians and non-Christians from several tribes. The two sisters of the Congregation who went there to teach the girls lived in a bark shelter at first. Later they would have a house and later still they would live in one of the stone towers of the fort. The work of the sisters at this mission was much praised by the colonial authorities. Because the Native girls could remain with their families, many problems that arose when attempts were made to educate them in boarding schools were avoided. Marguerite would have preferred to go further in her adaptation to the culture and way of life of the Native Peoples but royal policy at that time made this impossible. Soon, however, the school would have as teacher a Congregation sister of Huron and Iroquois descent.

New missions, new members

Since the early 1660s, Marie Raisin had been undertaking a travelling mission to the Trois-Rivières area. In 1666, she had wondered whether she was not called to a more traditional form of religious life and went to try out that vocation in the Ursuline cloister in Quebec. This experience confirmed her in her vocation to Marguerite's Congregation to which she returned after a few months. Her return was the occasion of much joy in Montreal especially to Marguerite Bourgeoys who must have wondered whether her Montreal community was to disappear, as had the earlier attempt in Troyes. Marie Raisin was a sister in whom she had great confidence. She had replaced Marguerite during her absence from 1670-72 and had supervised the completion of the new house. In 1676, she founded at Champlain the first Congregation mission off the island of Montreal.

Drawing by S.Sainte-Marthe-de-Béthanie, around 1940.

Still another permanent mission of the Congregation came into being in 1678, this time at Pointe-aux-Trembles on the eastern end of the island of Montreal where settlement had at last become safe. Wherever the sisters went, they not only taught the children but also gave what one of the intendants described as "touching and useful talks to the older women."

Not only was the Congregation undergoing geographical expansion at this time, it was also expanding its membership. The first Canadians to enter the Congregation were the Gariépy sisters from Château-Richer. They were folllowed by two aboriginal women: Marie-Thérèse Gannensagouas and Marie-Barbe Atontinon. Marie-Thérèse was the granddaughter of a Huron, François Thoronhiongo, who had been baptized by Saint Jean-de-Brébeuf and had maintained his Christian faith during two decades of captivity among the Iroquois.

After the establishment of peace in the late 1660s, Thoronhiongo came with several of his descendants to the native village where the Mountain Mission would one day be established. Among those with him was Gannensagouas who, in 1672, was officially adopted by Courcelle, the governor of New France, and given the queen's name, Marie-Thérèse. Courcelle also settled a sum of money on her to serve as her marriage dowry. When the time came, however,

Marie-Thérèse elected to join the sisters of the Congregation who had raised her, rather than to marry. At a time when it was believed in some quarters that the Native Peoples were not yet ready to be anything but receivers, it is notable that she became one of the teachers of her own people at the Mountain Mission.

Less is known of the life of the other Native sister, Marie-Barbe Atontinon d'Anotais. She was a member of the Onendaga tribe who had come to the Mountain Mission in 1676; she was received as a candidate in the Congregation in 1679. By the end of the decade, the Congregation had also received its first Montrealer of European parentage, Marie Barbier, youngest daughter of Gilbert Barbier, the carpenter who had helped Marguerite re-erect the cross on the mountain soon after her arrival in New France.

A dream realized

The 1670s also saw the fulfilment of a hope Marguerite had been cherishing for more than twenty years, the completion of the little pilgrimage chapel dedicated to Our Lady. In 1678, Notre-Dame-de-Bon-Secours became the first stone church on the island of Montreal. The statue given by the Baron de Fancamp received a place of honour. "Many marvels were accomplished by the prayers that were said in that chapel," Marguerite wrote. Very fittingly and like swords becoming ploughshares, a broken cannon given earlier by Maisonneuve was transformed into a bell for the new chapel. The first stone chapel was destroyed by fire in 1754 just before the war that brought the French regime in Canada to an end. It was rebuilt in the 1770s despite the difficulties of the time and still stands in Old Montreal. It continues to shelter the Baron de Fancamp's tiny statue and offers the pilgrim a haven of peace and quiet contemplation.

Last voyage to France

As the Congregation spread to new places and accepted new members, the question of maintaining unity became very important. For Marguerite, the foundation stone of a community is God "to whom we are inseparably joined". The Constitutions are "Our Lord Jesus Christ", his teachings and example. She believed that unity in the Congregation was above all a spiritual thing:

This union must be above all in our hearts and minds, for it is the same spirit of grace that has gathered us together and that ought to inspire us: a spirit of charity, of simplicity, of littleness, of poverty, of detachment from all things and surrender to God.

She wanted to see in her Congregation "the true spirit of cordiality and love that formed the glory and the beatitude of the first Christians." But she realized that the manner in which sisters of her community would follow Christ in the footsteps of Mary needed to be given more concrete expression. She understood too that the unity and stability of the Congregation required a Rule approved by Church authorities. Of course, the Congregation had not been living without a Rule prior to this time: Marguerite had brought with her to Canada the Rule that had been drawn up by Father Gendret in Troyes and approved by the theologians at the Sorbonne so many years before. This had been developed and modified in keeping with the experience of the young community. Now, however, it was necessary that the Rule be set down in a canonically acceptable form. Accordingly, Marguerite decided to go to France to consult other communities like her own, for several of these had just won approval. She could also consult Bishop Laval who had promised the Congregation a Rule and who was in Paris on business at this time.

Marguerite's other reason for wishing to go to France at this moment was not unconnected with the first reason: she hoped to obtain spiritual direction and advice from someone with whom she and her community were not already involved, someone who might give her enlightened and dispassionate counsel. Marguerite's generosity of spirit found sufficient the commandments of love of God and neighbour; that same generosity of spirit led her always to see the best in others "to excuse the intention if she cannot excuse the fault." She felt called to follow Christ in the practice of radical poverty. She writes that at his birth,

> He found no other house to shelter Him than a stable, no other cradle than a manger and straw for His bedding. During the course of His life, He had nowhere to rest; He died naked on the cross. His first instruction on the mountain was this: "Blessed are the poor in spirit."

She believed that the sisters of the Congregation, like the Apostles who "went without a purse or second tunic", should be ready to go out to teach even when "their livelihood was not assured." She was convinced that only through an absolute trust in God could they, like the Apostles, "work wonders". Now she had to deal with the fact that not all the women entering the Congregation had the same spiritual gifts as she. How could she reconcile her great dream for the Congregation with the human weaknesses of her companions? What was the best way to direct and guide and inspire them? Soon after her arrival in France, she recovered her peace through consultation with a Capuchin priest at La Rochelle, her port of entry. Her struggle with her questions and doubts was not over, however, as later events were to show.

Marguerite was now almost sixty years old and ill. When she reached Paris, she faced another challenge: the disapproval of Bishop Laval who not only told her sternly that she ought not to have come but forbade her to look for any new members for the Congregation in France. The bishop was himself in very low spirits due to the failure of his attempt to persuade the court to support him in his opposition to the trading of liquor to the Native Peoples. His plan for the organization of the Church in his diocese in a way that would prevent the inequalities of the Old World had also been rejected. It is perhaps understandable that he did not want to add an avant-garde community of women to his problems. Even as she later recalled her distress, Marguerite remembered with gratitude those who had been kind to her, especially Philip de Turmenye, who had been Maisonneuve's friend and who welcomed her and saw to her comfort, she says, as though she had been his sister.

Several good things emerged from this sojourn in Paris. Marguerite stayed with the Filles de la Croix, a newly founded uncloistered community, the first, in fact to have obtained letters patent. She was also introduced to Madame de Miramion, the superior and founder of another uncloistered community. Both these communities had Rules that she could examine. Since she was always more interested in practice than in theory, she could see for herself the application of those Rules, recognizing that they were written for a very different situation from the one she faced in Montreal. Marguerite made another important contact during her sojourn in Paris. This was Louis Tronson who had become superior of the Sulpicians in 1678. The impression she made on him then would cause him to give her his unfailing support in the difficult events that would mark the last decade of her life.

Even though Marguerite was not accompanied by any new recruits for the Congregation on her return journey, there were again other women aboard the ship who expected to marry and begin families in New France. And although she does not seem to have been called upon to care for the sick or the dying this time, she was asked to intervene in another crisis. When four enemy ships were sighted on the horizon, the passengers panicked and an appeal was made to Marguerite to establish calm. To the captain's relief she did so. " If we are captured," she told her fellow travellers, "we will be taken to Holland or to England

Detail of a drawing entitled "Papa Thibodeau" by S. Sainte-Marthe-de-Béthanie, around 1940.

and we will find God there since God is everywhere." The enemy ships disappeared from the horizon and the French ship was able to finish the voyage in safety. Marguerite was back in Montreal by the feast of the Assumption, patronal feast of her chapel of pilgrimage and the day on which Marie Barbier made her promises as a sister of the Congregation.

Trial by fire

The 1680s were to be an even greater period of expansion for the Congregation than were the 1670s with the first new mission being established in 1680 at Lachine in the western area of the island of Montreal. More Montrealers followed Marie Barbier into the community, among them Marguerite Le Moyne. Her mother was Mathurine Godé, the only small child among the founders of Montreal in 1642. Marguerite Bourgeoys recorded a touching story about Mathurine and her mother Françoise. In 1657, both their husbands were killed by the Iroquois, some of whom were captured. "The two widows came to beg that [the prisoners] would not be harmed and brought them some food." There were also other new arrivals from France.

But this was also a decade marked by disaster and loss. Surprisingly, given life expectancies of that time, until then there had been no deaths in the Congregation. The situation changed in the late summer of 1681 with the death of Madeleine Constantin who was one of the recruits of 1672 and only thirty-five years of age. Worse was to follow. Among the new Canadian members of the Congregation were Marie and Catherine Charly, daughters of Marie Dumesnil, the young girl confided to Marguerite's care on her first voyage to New France in 1653. Marie Charly died in April 1683 before reaching her twenty-first birthday. Despite these losses, the Congregation did take on another mission that summer, though it was to be of short duration. This was at the Jesuit Native mission at Sault-Saint-Louis (now Kahnawake). Then, at the end of the year, catastrophe struck: during the night of December 6-7, 1683, the Congregation house was totally destroyed by fire.

By far the worst loss in the fire was that of the lives of two of the sisters, Marguerite Sommillard, the eldest niece of Marguerite Bourgeoys, and Geneviève du Rosoy, another of the recruits of 1672. Geneviève was assistant superior and Marguerite Sommillard was bursar. Some sources claim that elections were to have been held in the Congregation on what turned out to be the day after the fire and that these two women had been regarded as the most likely candidates to succeed Marguerite Bourgeoys as superior. Whether or not she had been planning to resign as superior, Marguerite Bourgeoys certainly could not do so now, nor could she take time to indulge her grief.

At this moment, more than ever, her qualities of leadership were called upon, her courage, her hope, her conviction that God did indeed will the presence in Montreal and in New France of a group of women who would imitate the example of the Blessed Virgin during her life on earth. The bishop might think that, in the face of such a crushing material loss, the solution to the problems of the Congregation would be unification with the cloistered Ursulines in Quebec. And, if the Congregation was to survive, it was not only Marguerite's vision and her conviction that were called for, it was the practical qualities that would enable it to rise from the ashes and begin again.

So it was that when spring came in 1684, the sixty-four year old Marguerite threw herself whole-heartedly into the task of rebuilding. Charles Glandelet, her first biographer, tells us:

> Her courage ... was undaunted; it remained firm and generous ... It was not long before her confidence was rewarded. Divine Providence raised up charitable persons who provided the means to build an even larger, better, and more suitable house than the first.

The most complete statement about the fire and its aftermath is to be found in the report of Quebec's second bishop in his report after his first visit to the Congregation:

> It is a marvel that they were able to survive after the accident that happened to them three or four years ago; their whole house was burned in one night; they saved neither their furniture nor their clothes, only too happy to save their lives, still two of them perished in the flames. The courage of those who escaped sustained them in their extreme poverty; and though they were more than thirty in number, divine Providence provided for their pressing necessities. It seemed that this calamity served only to make them more virtuous and more helpful to their neighbour; for there is no good that they have not undertaken since then.

A new bishop, new challenges

Although some years younger than Marguerite, Bishop Laval was feeling the effects of age and ill health. Given the immensity of his diocese and the magnitude of the problems it faced, he decided that the time had come for a younger and more vigorous bishop. His chosen successor was Jean-Baptiste de La Croix de Chevrières de Saint-Vallier who was just thirty-one years old and filled with both energy and zeal when he arrived at Quebec in 1685 as Vicar General. The following spring the bishop-elect set off to tour his diocese even before the ice had completely melted from the waterways. He was greatly impressed by the Congregation when he visited Montreal and by one of its works in particular.

Besides the schools, the work on the missions, both travelling and permanent, and the teaching of the older women, the Congregation had also undertaken the organization of a workshop where poor women could come to learn the skills that would help them earn their living. Both the civil and the religious authorities saw this as one of the most important works of the community. Through the generosity of the Sulpicians, women in need who came to learn in the workshop could be offered not only instruction but also their meals. It was a work very dear to the heart of Marguerite herself. To teach people how to do "honourable work" and so permit them to retain their self-respect and maintain themselves and their families was always one of her most important aims. The bishop wanted to see the Congregation established in the Quebec region as soon as possible.

The first new mission in that area was founded in 1685 at Sainte-Famille on Île d'Orléans by the young Marie Barbier and Anne Meyrand, one of the more recent arrivals from France. Marie Barbier's account of their November journey down the Saint Lawrence and of the hardships of their first winter lodged with the family of one of the colonists gives considerable insight into the sacrifices and privations demanded of those following the *vie voyagère*, the life of travel in the footsteps of Mary. These included not just danger, hunger, cold and loneliness but also something even more painful for someone of Marie Barbier's temperament, a complete lack of privacy. They were forced to live in the already crowded houses of the local settlers. The following spring, the bishop called Marie Barbier to Quebec to open yet another mission. Since he had been especially impressed with the work done by the Congregation for the poor women of Montreal, he now wanted them to do something similar in Quebec.

As Marie Barbier's account shows, important decisions about opening new missions and staffing them were normally made then in a democratic manner in the Congregation. It is unclear how much Bishop Saint-Vallier consulted Marguerite Bourgeoys or the community about moving the sisters or opening new houses. It is possible that he even sent off a sister of the Congregation alone to Port-Royal in what is now Nova Scotia. Marguerite was always ready to respond to the wishes of her bishop and the needs of the Church. She believed firmly that we are obliged not only to love our neighbour but also to keep our neighbour in the love the neighbour owes us. However, balancing the demands of the bishop with maintaining unity in the Congregation required all her tact and several journeys to Quebec that became more and more difficult as she aged and conditions became more and more dangerous.

The Quebec assignment that caused the most difficulty to the Congregation was that of opening a *hôpital général*. Such institutions were not hospitals in the modern sense of the term. Rather they were founded to care for orphans, widows, the aged, the handicapped, those suffering from chronic disease, in fact, for all the poor who were incapable of looking after themselves and who might otherwise be begging in the street. At first there had been no need for such institutions in New France with its very small and mainly young and vigorous population. By the closing years of the century, this was no longer true and in

1689, the bishop decided to turn the house he had given the Congregation to use as a school for girls into Quebec's *hôpital général* and to employ sisters of the Congregation to run it. A group of old men became its first inhabitants. Once again the bishop intervened in the assignment of the sisters. This was neither a work for which the Congregation had been founded nor one for which their letters patent authorized it. Eventually, the bishop replaced them with the sisters of the Quebec Hôtel-Dieu and the sisters of the Congregation were able to direct their efforts to their school established in the Lower Town.

Beginning of a tumultuous decade

The relative peace New France had enjoyed since the arrival of the Carignan-Salières regiment came to an end in 1689. The causes lay partly in Europe, where France was once more at war with England and Holland, but also in conflicts involving the fur trade in North America where French colonists fought English colonists and Native allies of the French fought Native allies of the English. Hostilities opened in Montreal with the event known as the Lachine Massacre in August of that year. For most of the next decade there was war, and atrocities were committed by both sides.

This was a war that deeply touched those close to Marguerite and all the Canadian-born members of the Congregation. Marguerite's niece Catherine was on mission at Lachine at the time of the massacre and brought the orphaned children with her to the Congregation house in what is now Old Montreal. Catherine's sister Louise was widowed at this time, most likely as a consequence of the war. Other members of the Congregation lost brothers, brothers-in-law and cousins in the fighting. Once more it was a time of grief and terror.

It is probably not surprising that the disturbance of the time gave rise to a very strange movement in Montreal. Early in November 1689, Marguerite Tardy, a sister of the Congregation who had come from France a few years earlier, approached Marguerite Bourgeoys. Sister Tardy told Marguerite Bourgeoys that, as she had watched by the fire the night before, a sister who had died sixteen months earlier told her, "I have been sent by God. Tell the Superior of the Congregation that she is in the state of mortal sin …" Two months later Sister Tardy returned with another message: "This Superior has still not done what she ought to do. This is the last time I will warn her, for I am going to heaven." So began an unprecedented period of anguish for Marguerite Bourgeoys.

"This caused me great suffering, more than I can say"

To understand the reaction of Marguerite Bourgeoys to the accusations of Sister Tardy, it is necessary to have a sense of the climate of the time and the circumstances amid which her accusations were made. The parish priest of Ville-Marie was preaching from the pulpit that the horror and misfortunes of the war had come upon the people as a result of their sins and of their infidelity to the ideals that had led to the founding of Montreal in the first place. They were told that it was time for a great movement of reform, for a return to the inspiration of the founders. Sister Tardy was seen in many quarters as a chosen instrument of God to bring this about. She had supporters at the Congregation, at the Hôtel-Dieu and among the ordinary faithful of Montreal. Most important, she had the support of three Sulpicians, the most influential of them Joseph de La Colombière.

Joseph was the younger brother of Claude de La Colombière who, just a few years before, had been the spiritual director of Saint Margaret Mary Alacoque.

Saint Margaret Mary had experienced a series of visions connected to the promotion of devotion to the Sacred Heart of Jesus. Abbé Joseph de la Colombière had shown such promise that he had been sent to Montreal in the expectation that he would one day be superior there. He was very well respected in New France by both clergy and devout laity and also enjoyed the confidence and esteem of the bishop.

Sister Tardy and her supporters formulated a plan to unite the Sulpicians, the Congregation and the hospital nuns in a single reformed community. This was linked to the devotion to the Holy Family associated with the foundation of Montreal: the Sulpicians would represent Jesus, the sisters of the Congregation, Mary, and the hospital nuns, Saint Joseph, their patron. Not just Marguerite Bourgeoys, but also François Dollier de Casson, superior of the Sulpicians, and Catherine Maçé, the superior at the Hôtel-Dieu, were under attack.

Marguerite was now seventy years old and had just lived through a very difficult decade. The Congregation had suffered not only the devastation of the fire in 1683 but also the deaths of eight sisters, many of them the young Canadians. The fault of which Sister Tardy accused Marguerite Bourgeoys was laxness. Now she could only ask herself if her gentleness, her desire to lead by inspiring, by acting as a "torch" rather than by judging and correcting, were the cause of the failures she could see in the Congregation and beyond it. She feared that she had indeed been guilty of "negligence, of lack of firmness in promoting the spiritual advancement of the sisters". She questioned her own motivation. Had she been seeking only to be liked?

Marguerite entered into a period of darkness of spirit that, she later wrote, lasted fifty months, a period in which she did indeed begin to feel that she was in a state of mortal sin. She describes herself as becoming "sadder and less sociable." For four months she did not receive Communion; after that she did so only at the insistence of her confessor. "This is my greatest suffering," she wrote, "for in my great need to pray I am without fervour." Finally, she asked the bishop to accept her resignation because, she said in what are perhaps the saddest words in her writings: "During these trying times, I found by certain signs that my sisters had lost the confidence they used to have in me and that I had lost the freedom to speak to them." Her sense of loneliness and isolation can only have been increased by the deaths of two of her original companions, Marie Raisin in 1691 and Anne Hioux in 1693. Now, of the original members of the Congregation, only Catherine Crolo was left with Marguerite.

"I will always hope in Him"

Throughout these years, Marguerite continued to perform her duties as superior. She made a last trip to Quebec where she had to regulate a difficult business affair for the Congregation. The sisters had made a mistake in a business agreement and had contracted a debt they could not meet on time. The creditor was indignant. Marguerite remained sensitive to the rights and needs of those around her. Her main concern was that the Congregation should act with justice toward those with whom they were doing business. At the same time, she wanted to be sure that the sisters travelling in the Quebec region would have a place of refuge and rest. She prayed and found a way to act justly and to provide for the sisters.

Her relations with the sisters at Montreal are reflected in the reminiscences of Marguerite Trottier who entered the Congregation with her sister Catherine in 1692. She described the moment when she and her sister took the habit. Marguerite Bourgeoys, she writes, was still superior. She laid her hand gently on the head of each of them in turn, bidding them affectionately to remain always little and humble "like cabbages and pumpkins." When the two made their promises in the Congregation, it was decided that Marguerite Trottier would go on mission to Château-Richer while Catherine who was less robust would stay in Montreal. Marguerite Bourgeoys noticed that Marguerite Trottier was much grieved to be leaving her sister. She encouraged the young woman by communicating her own vision of the work of education as a participation in the redeeming work of Christ. She used a powerful image she had seen traced in a stained glass window in the cathedral of Troyes, that of a gathering up of the drops of the blood flowing from the wounds of the crucified Christ. Not only was Marguerite Trottier comforted by these words, they continued all her life to be a source of strength and to inspire her in her dealings with her pupils.

Throughout all this time and despite everything, Marguerite did not lose hope in God. She wrote, "Even though I cannot refuse to recognize my unfortunate state, I have never doubted the mercy of God. I will always hope in Him, even when I see myself with one foot in hell." Her pain did not end even when the three Sulpicians involved were recalled to France and Sister Tardy departed with them, thus resolving the situation in Montreal. Instead, relief came as unexpectedly as the touch of grace in 1640. Marguerite was relieved "as suddenly as darkness is penetrated by light when a window is opened. I cannot explain it otherwise."

The question of the Rule

Marguerite Bourgeoys was succeeded as superior by Marie Barbier in the elections held in 1693. The first Montrealer to have entered the Congregation, Marie was the only one to have already attained the age of thirty. The others elected to major office were also women with deep roots in Montreal. Catherine Charly who was elected assistant superior was a daughter of Marie Dumesnil. Marguerite Le Moyne was elected mistress of novices. The bursar, Marguerite Garièpy, was also Canadian born.

The young and inexperienced council soon had very serious difficulties to face. In 1694, Bishop Saint-Vallier presented the Congregation with a Rule that he himself had compiled. While it did incorporate some of the practices already in use in the Congregation, it was much drawn from the rules of older communities, most of them cloistered. When the sisters of the Congregation pointed out that many of the prescriptions of this new Rule would make their manner of life and their work impossible, the bishop said he would simply dispense them from those provisions. When they continued to raise objections, he became angry and threatened to impose cloister on them at once and to prevent them from receiving any new candidates into the community.

There was a fundamental difference between the way in which Bishop Saint-Vallier perceived the Congregation's way of life and their own vision of its significance. The bishop was very happy to have at his disposal a group of women whom he could call on to travel and to undertake various works in his diocese but he believed that the need was temporary, a condition of the times. As New France became more settled, he thought, the need for such a group would disappear and the Congregation would settle down in the cloister, perhaps as part of one of the already existing communities. He could not conceive of the fact that their uncloistered state, the freedom to go out to carry Christ wherever they were needed, was part of their essence.

The council of the Congregation urgently needed all of Marguerite's strength, vision and tact to cope with this challenge. And, at the age of seventy-four, she poured them forth as generously as she had always done. Some good came out of this crisis. For one thing, it healed whatever wounds remained in the Congregation as a result of the Sister Tardy affair. More important, it made Marguerite put into writing her vision for the community and its inspiration. To do this, she revisited the events of her own life, an experience that helped her perceive more clearly the working out of the plan of God in that life and renewed her courage, her hope, her conviction.

For Marguerite, the most serious fault of the new Rule was its failure to describe the basic inspiration of the Congregation. To articulate that vision, Marguerite began by telling two stories. One was that of the young girl who was touched by grace on Rosary Sunday in 1640 and began the attempt to found a community that would live as Mary had done when she was on earth. The other was that of a group of people who, at the same time, were planning to establish a missionary colony on the far-off island of Montreal. The stories came together thirteen years later when the girl from the Rosary procession found the banner that convinced her that Mary had been saving a place for her in Montreal from the beginning.

Marguerite's approach was positive. She described who her sisters were: women like the Blessed Virgin ready "to undertake any journey on which there was good to be done or some work of charity to be performed." Marguerite explained that in the early Christian Church, the Blessed Virgin "gave all her care to the establishing and strengthening of the Church. She taught the first Christians to know and love Our Lord in every way she could, never refusing to go anywhere that charity or need called her." And, Marguerite concluded, "We wish to follow her in some way."

At the same time, like Mary, the sisters would preserve "an inner solitude", pondering Christ's words in their hearts, conscious always of the presence of God, especially in all with whom they worked. They would be most at home among the poor.

It was also important to Marguerite that the poor would be able to join and be at home in the Congregation. For this to be possible, Marguerite objected to two provisions in the new Rule. The first was the exaction of a dowry from women entering the community. The second was the provision for two categories of sisters, one that could both vote and hold major office and the other that could vote but not hold office. "The sisters should be equal," she wrote. "After her resignation, the superior can be the cook or serve in any other capacity of which she is thought capable." As Mary had lived and worked among the first Christians, the sisters were not to keep themselves apart from the ordinary faithful but would worship in the parish church and find their directors among the parish clergy. Even in death, they would not be separated from the rest of the faithful but would be buried in the parish church.

The struggle over the Rule continued for more than four years during three of which the bishop was absent in France. Marguerite and the Congregation received much help from Abbé Louis Tronson in Paris even though his health and sight were failing. Finally, a compromise was reached. Many of the elements in the Rule most objectionable to the Congregation were removed, but Marguerite's description of her inspiration in the life of Mary, especially in her Visitation and in her role in the post-Pentecostal Church, was not incorporated. It had, however, been given expression in the writings Marguerite would leave behind and would live on in the Congregation as a spirit to be communicated from one generation to the next even if it had found no place in the written Rule.

Jeanne Le Ber

Marguerite found consolation during these years in something she saw as yet another sign of the working out of God's designs in the Congregation. During the night of February 24-25, 1695, the Hôtel-Dieu in Montreal was totally destroyed by fire. The members of the Congregation responded at once as the neighbouring community had done for them a little over a decade before. They offered a temporary home to the hospital nuns who remained until November. That same summer, the Congregation also became home to a woman whose unique vocation was and still is a cause of wonder. This was Jeanne Le Ber.

Jeanne was born in Montreal in 1662, the only daughter of Jacques Le Ber who became one of the wealthiest men in New France and Jeanne Le Moyne, member of one of its most illustrious families. Her godparents were Maisonneuve and Jeanne Mance. She was sent to the Ursuline boarding school in Quebec at the age of twelve and the anticipation was that on her return she would make a brilliant marriage. Instead, she embraced a life of asceticism and intense prayer. At the age of eighteen, she received permission to enter into reclusion in her parents' house which she left only to attend Mass. Jeanne was fervently devoted to Christ in the Blessed

(Detail) Pall embroidered by Jeanne Le Ber. The religious recluse embroidered vestments and altar ornaments. Photo: Pierre Guzzo, Maison Saint-Gabriel

Sacrament, to the Blessed Virgin and to the angels. Her days were spent in prayer and in the embroidering of liturgical vestments of exceptional artistry and beauty, as well as in the more practical fashioning of clothing for the poor.

In the early 1690s, she proposed the building of a chapel for the Congregation with an apartment attached to the sanctuary where she could live and continue her life of constant adoration. On August 5, 1695, at the close of a public ceremony that marked her act as belonging to the universal Church, Jeanne entered into permanent reclusion in this apartment. When questioned later about what had attracted her to such a way of life, her only answer was to open the tiny doorway that separated her from the chapel and to point to the tabernacle sheltering the Blessed Sacrament saying, "There is my magnet."

The day of her entry into her apartment gave immense joy to Marguerite Bourgeoys. Jeanne's presence at the Congregation while the Hôtel-Dieu nuns were also there meant that the three states of religious women described to Marguerite so many years before by Father Gendret, Mary Magdalen, Martha and Mary, the mother of Jesus, were altogether "in the house of the Blessed Virgin." In this, she saw another "sign" confirming the authenticity of the inspiration of the Congregation.

Lydia Longley and Mary Sayward

The Congregation also saw other unexpected arrivals in the last years of Marguerite's life. As the war continued, it was the custom of the Native allies of the French to bring to Montreal captives taken in raids on the English colonies and offer them for ransom. One of these captives was Lydia Longley whose whole family, with the exception of one brother and of a little sister who died on the dreadful journey up to Montreal, had been massacred in a raid on Deerfield, Massachusetts. Lydia found refuge in the household of Jacques Le Ber while his daughter Jeanne still lived there. The young woman decided not to be repatriated when the opportunity came but to remain in Montreal and to convert to Catholicism. Tradition says that it was Marguerite Bourgeoys herself who instructed Lydia in the Catholic faith. By special permission, she was received into the Church in the Congregation chapel rather than in the parish church so that Jeanne Le Ber, now in reclusion there, could witness the ceremony.

Lydia became a sister of the Congregation as did Mary Sayward, another former captive from the English colonies who had been given refuge at the Congregation with her mother and sister. The Congregation had now numbered among its members women from each of the groups to be found in the northern part of

North America at that time: French women, Canadian descendants of the French settlers, women from the Native Peoples and women of English descent. They were able to live and work together in peace while the groups from which they came were engaged in a war with one another. In this manner they demonstrated the truth of one of Marguerite's most cherished beliefs: "When difficulties come along, there are always enough charitable people to bring about a reconciliation."

Marguerite du Saint-Sacrement

Bishop Saint-Vallier returned from France in 1697. The following spring, he sent to Montreal a revised version of the Rule of 1694. In June, he himself arrived in Montreal and held several days of meetings with the Congregation, meetings in which Marguerite played an active role, lending her vital support to Marie Barbier and her council. On June 24, the twenty-four members of the Congregation at Montreal who were well enough to do so signed their acceptance of the Rule and the next day pronounced vows of poverty, chastity, obedience and commitment to the education of persons of their sex. The sisters on mission in Quebec followed their example a few days later. They also took religious names, often the addition of the name of a patron saint or a mystery to their baptismal names.

Marguerite Bourgeoys chose the name Marguerite du Saint-Sacrement, Marguerite of the Blessed Sacrament. On July 2, feast of the Visitation, she and the other sisters made their vows perpetual. Although the problems related to the preservation of its founding charism were not over, the Congrégation de Notre-Dame de Montréal now had official status within the Church that gave it considerably increased security and stability.

"All the desires I feel come to an end gently"

In the elections that immediately followed the acceptance of the Rule and pronunciation of vows, Marguerite Le Moyne replaced the ailing Marie Barbier as superior of the Congregation. She and Catherine Charly, who was also elected to the council, would continue to lead the community until almost the middle of the following century. A descendant of the founders of 1642 like Marie Barbier, Marguerite Le Moyne would soon prove herself capable of preserving the unity and integrity of the Congregation.

These last years of the life of Marguerite Bourgeoys were gentle years. Outside, the war was drawing to a close and the Great Peace would be signed in Montreal in 1701. For Marguerite Bourgeoys, it was a time for last good-byes

This portrait of Marguerite Bourgeoys was painted by Pierre Le Ber at the time of her death in 1700. Subsequently overpainted and restored in 1962. Photo : Normand Rajotte and for the final surrender into the hands of her loving God. She wrote once, "Our good God has given me this grace: that all the desires I feel come to an end gently." Marguerite was living, Sister Marie Morin wrote, "so humble and retired that just the sight of her inspires the love of humility."

Although not confined to the infirmary, Marguerite often went there to take her meals with Catherine Crolo, the last and oldest of her friends. Sister Morin had described Catherine in 1697 as "indefatigable for work ... living today, aged over eighty, in great odour of virtue." However, at the end of February 1699, Sister Crolo died. In October 1699, Catherine Sommillard, Marguerite's youngest niece, died at the age of only forty-four, "worn out", says the history of the Congregation, "with the demands of missionary life." Then, on the morning of New Year's Eve 1699, Marguerite was awakened with the news that Catherine Charly, the mistress of novices, just thirty-three years old, was so seriously ill that her death seemed imminent. As the daughter of Marie Dumesnil, the first bride she had helped establish in the New World, Catherine was almost like a granddaughter to Marguerite Bourgeoys.

"She died, my dear sisters, as she had lived"

When Marguerite heard this threatening news, her first response was to turn to God. She is reported to have asked God why He would take this young woman who could still accomplish so much in the community rather than herself who was now old and useless. Since her own health began to deteriorate and that of Catherine Charly to improve from that moment on, her words have traditionally been interpreted as an offering of her life for Catherine's sake. But the words also have another significance.

Marguerite had worried a great deal about her young sisters, about the depth of their insight into the charism of the community, about their capacity for the sacrifices and strength and courage needed to carry it on. Her words indicate a final renunciation: a willingness to give over into their hands the community she had spent so much of her life building. They express her confidence in the members of the Congregation she was leaving behind. Ultimately, they express her abandonment not only of herself but also of her Congregation into the hands of God.

Even as her physical sufferings increased, she found time for gratitude and gentle laughter: she teased her attendants that they were taking such good care of her that it did not seem that they wanted her to go to heaven. She found time for joy, singing hymns and asking the sisters to sing with her. All the anguish of the first years of the preceding decade was gone. Finally, on the morning of January 12, 1700, she died "as she had lived," wrote Marguerite Le Moyne, "loving God with her whole heart and manifesting an ardent desire to be with her Creator."

Saint Marguerite of Canada

There was no doubt in the minds of all those whose lives she had touched that in Marguerite Bourgeoys they had known a saint. When she was buried the next day in the parish church as she would have wished, her funeral was one of the largest New France had yet known. "If the saints were canonized today as they were in olden times by the voice of the people and of the clergy," wrote one of those in attendance, "tomorrow we would celebrate the Mass of Saint Marguerite of Canada." In fact, many years would pass before that would become possible. Marguerite was declared Venerable by Pope Leo XIII on December 7, 1878 and beatified by Pope Pius XII on November 12, 1950. Finally, on October 31, 1982, she was canonized by Pope John Paul II in Saint Peter's Basilica in Rome.

Detail of a portrait of Marguerite Bourgeoys by Charles Vinh, 2008.
Photo: Normand Rajotte.

Since 2005, her tomb has lain in Notre-Dame-de-Bon-Secours Chapel in Montreal beneath the altar where the tiny statue Marguerite carried across the ocean is enshrined. There, people from all over the world come to pray for her intercession for, across the centuries, many women and men have continued to find in her a confidante, a source of strength and hope and a friend, as well as an inspiring example. They come also to learn more about her in the museum attached to Notre-Dame-de-Bon-Secours Chapel or at the Maison Saint-Gabriel, which occupies the old farmhouse in Pointe-Saint-Charles.

The Congrégation de Notre-Dame

Marguerite's Congregation has endured. As in her time, it has remained open to journeying like Mary wherever there is "good to be done or some work of charity to be performed." Sisters of her community can now be found in Canada, in the

United States, in Japan, in Central America, in France and in Cameroon. And, as in Marguerite's time, women from all these countries have joined the Congregation. They undertake the work of "liberating education" in the many forms this may take in their own time and place. Many other women and men, attracted by her charism, have become Associates of the Congregation. As the opening prayer of the Mass of Saint Marguerite Bourgeoys requests, they attempt, "to proclaim the loving presence of the Word made flesh among us." This is a fitting tribute to the heroic woman who wrote: "All I have ever desired and what I still most ardently wish is that the great precept of the love of God above all things and of the neighbour as oneself be written in every heart."

ACHEVÉ D'IMPRIMER SUR LES PRESSES
DE L'IMPRIMERIE TRANSCONTINENTAL
AU MOIS JUIN 2009
QUÉBEC (CANADA)